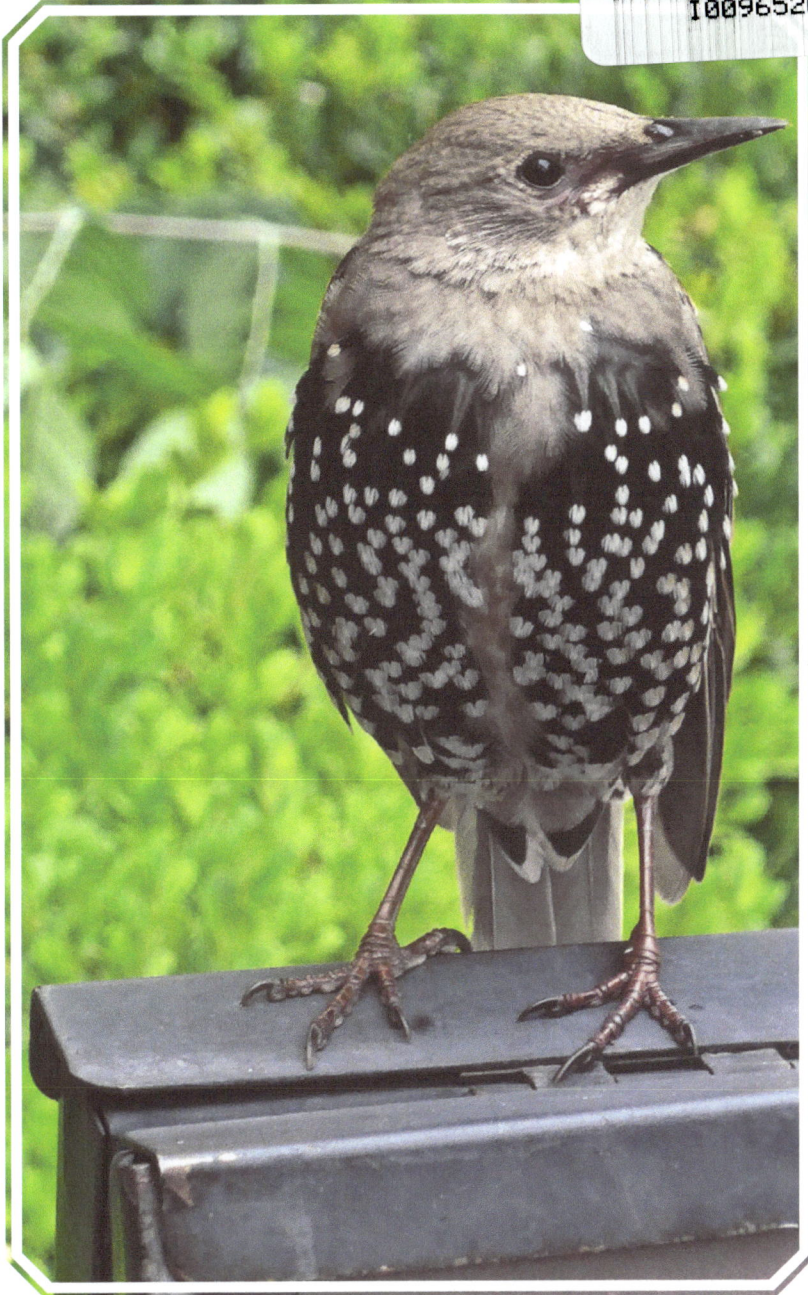

Proverbs

on

Animals,

Plants

and Nature

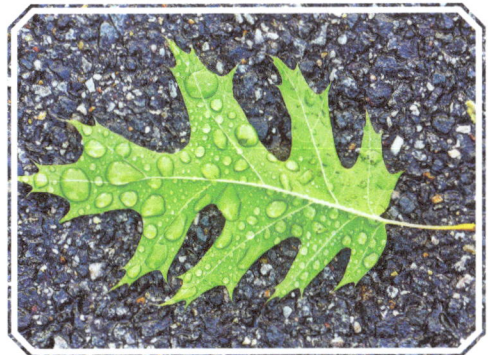

Proverbs on Animals, Plants and Nature
Noël-Marie Fletcher
© December 2020, Fletcher & Co. Publishers LLC

Author, editor and compiled by: Noël-Marie Fletcher
Interior design & type: Noël-Marie Fletcher
Cover design: Zita Steele
Cover and interior illustrations: Noël-Marie Fletcher

Cataloging-in-Publication data for this book is available from the Library of Congress.

Library of Congress Control Number: 2020941755

Cataloging information
ISBN-13 978-1-941184-36-3

First Edition
Published in the United States of America

All photos were taken by Noël-Marie Fletcher, who can always be found with a camera in hand, except for these images taken by her daughter Zita Ballinger Fletcher—an author and military historian whose pen name is Zita Steele. Zita's photos are: bats p. 8, donkey p. 27, elephants pp. 28–29, owls p. 58, snakes pp. 72–74, middle cloud p. 80, wolves. pp. 94–95, and caterpillar p. 96.

Proverbs

on

Animals,

Plants

and Nature

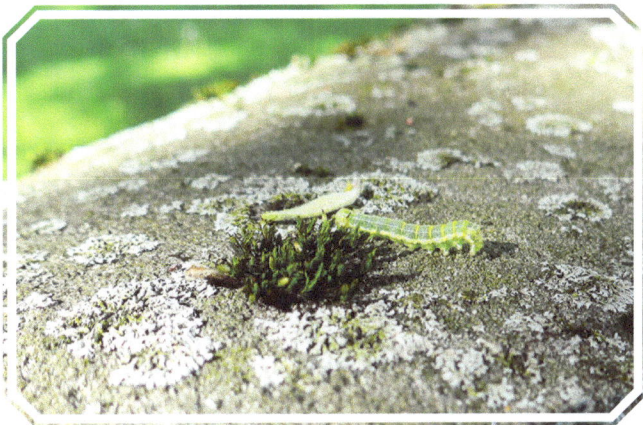

Collected and arranged
by Noël-Marie Fletcher

with her photography &
illustrations

FLETCHER & CO. PUBLISHERS
www.fletcherpublishers.com

Contents

Without ascending the mountain,
we cannot admire the height of heaven; without descending into the valley,
we cannot admire the depth of the earth;
without listening to the maxims
left by the ancients,
we cannot know the excellence of wisdom.
—Chinese

This Book

Wildlife, nature and various types of pets have been part of my life since my earliest years. I was born and grew up in an agricultural greenbelt near the famous Rio Grande in an area known as the North Valley due to its many orchards, alfalfa fields, ditches, and vineyards. My maternal forefathers lived near the banks of the Rio Grande since the 1600s when they came to New Mexico as Spanish conquistadors. The fabric of my life is interwoven with the elegant beauty of nature and the simple innocence of creatures around me.

Daytime in my youth was serenaded by meadowlarks and mockingbirds singing above the fields. Cicadas buzzed on trees. Summer winds brought waves of warmth tinged with a delicate sweet scent of newly cut alfalfa. Muddy water murmured as it lapped the sides of ditch banks. Brooding gray clouds heralded the crisp aroma of afternoon rain showers. At night, crickets and toads exchanged duets occasionally punctuated by shrieking yips from wandering coyotes. Fiery orange, pink and yellow hues at sunset splashed above horizons. Midnight skies were awash with shimmering stars appearing so close to earth (there it's nearly a mile above sea level), it seemed you could reach out to touch them. Sometimes a silent barn owl flying over the mesa suddenly whooshed

Scenes from the North Valley where I grew up.

past under the bright glow of a moon.

An awareness of plants, animals, the seasons, the sky, the wind, the mountains, and stars remains with me today no matter where I am. Often my photographs reflect my awareness of my natural surroundings.

As a writer and avid reader, I enjoy discovering wisdom passed down through the ages in proverbs. I have an interest in and admiration for different cultures. I've been fortunate to experience living in different countries and knowing people of various ethnicities. Thus, my combined interests shaped this collection of proverbs. Making these selections, which came primarily came from books, I learned about how different cultures share wisdom with the animals kingdom and nature within their surroundings. No disparaging intent should be inferred from the use of some male pronouns from eras predating today's political correctness. No offense is meant. I've revised some to be more gender neutral and have included the language of origin when possible.

Lastly, it should be obvious that I'm an animal lover. Some of my best friends in my lifetime have been my pets. I've had a many personal experiences with animals as my

Me as a teen holding Junior.

My beloved cat Funny Face.

pets or shared family ones — from a peacock to goats, a sparrow hawk, a screech owl, geese, ducks, a guinea hen, and Netherland dwarf bunnies to parakeets, fish, dogs and cats. Most of these pets were rescues — like the peacock found wandering in a rugged mountain range by hunters, a wild Mexican duck flying overhead who spotted friendly geese in the backyard and decided to stay, an abused cattle dog limping in a neighborhood with a hurt foot and no identification. I have included some of their photos among these pages so they can live on and be shared with others.

My guinea hen Piccolo.

My goose Jill, left, with her brother Pepino.

Joselito the sparrow hawk.

Ant

A thousand ants can carry an earthworm so the words of many can change a lie into a truth. — *Bengali*

In the ant's house, a little dew makes a deluge. — *Persian*

A little trickle of water is a flood to an ant.

The bees have kings and ministers; ants have father and son; all creatures assent to the social relations. — *Chinese*

You can sooner detect an ant moving upon black earth on a dark night than all the motions of pride in your heart. — *Persian*

The sleep of kings is an anthill. — *Pashto*

Every ant has its ire. — *Portuguese*

Ape

The ape can speak but it does not cease to be a beast. — *Chinese*

Apes remains apes though you clothe them in velvet. — *German*

An old ape has an old eye.

An old ape never made a pretty face.

The higher an ape climbs, the more he shows his bald haunches. — *French*

The baboon, in the eyes of its mother, is a gazelle. — *Arabic*

Bat

A bat hanging upside down laughs at the topsy-turvy world. — *Japanese*

For every fruit eaten by a bat, a hundred are spoiled. — *Tamil*

Bats are found in groups.

Bats devour by striking, squirrels by nibbling. — *Tamil*

If the bat cannot see in the daylight is it the fault of the sun? — *Persian*

Suspicions among thoughts are like bats among birds.

Where there are no birds, the bat will be king. — *Japanese*

Bear

The bear wants a tail and cannot be a lion.

If the bear will learn to dance, he must go to school early. — *German*

If you go after a bear, take some straw; if you go after a wild boar, drag a coffin with you. — *Russian*

Bear and bull catch no fox. — *German*

Friendship with a fool is like a bear's embrace. — *Persian*

A bear's friendship is to scratch and tear. — *Urdu*

The bear that is hungry never dances. — *Turkish*

Bee

The good bee sips not a fallen flower. — *Chinese*

Where bees are, there is honey.

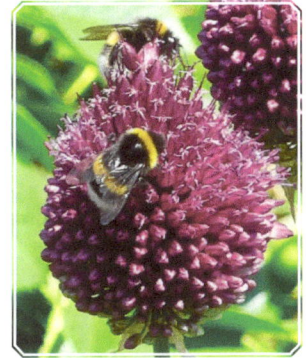

Bees wish for flowers, good men for what is virtuous, flies for what is putrid, bad men for blemishes in others. — *Burmese*

We should use a book as a bee does a flower.

Honey is sweet but the bee stings. — *Italian*

One bee is better than a thousand flies. — *German*

Say to the austere and uncivil bee, when you cannot afford honey, do not sting. — *Persian*

The bee stings a weeping face. — *Japanese*

Don't approach bees without having your head covered. — *Turkish*

Bees that have honey in their mouths have stings in their tails.

Do as the bee does with the rose, take the honey and leave the thorn. — *German*

Bees don't make honey in the moonlight. — *Hindi*

The strength of the bee is its patience. — *Welsh*

A bee does not touch a withered flower. — *Swedish*

The king of bees has no sting. — *Portuguese*

Beetle

The beetle is a beauty in the eyes of its mother.

As beetles smell the fragrance of flowers at a distance so too the learned person understands another's character at a distance. — *Tamil*

The beetle in its hole is a sultan. — *Arabic*

There is no tree that cannot be bored by a beetle. — *Tamil*

Birds

Birds will leave to go to lofty trees. — *Chinese*

Birds pay equal honors to all people.

Every bird needs its own feathers. — *German*

A bird is known by its note, and a man by his talk.

One cannot fly without wings. — *French*

Birds of a feather flock together.

Fine feathers make fine birds. — *Russian*

Every bird is known by its feathers.

An old bird is not caught with chaff.

Cuckoos, though they may dwell in the companionship with cranes, never cease from their sweet notes for song.

The female bird builds the nest. — *Turkish*

Every bird must hatch her own egg.

'Tis an ill bird that betrays its own nest.

Little by little, the bird builds the nest. —*German*

A little bird only needs a little nest.

Where the nest and eggs are, the birds are near.— *German*

Every bird likes its own nest the best.

Where the birds build their nests, there they sleep.

It is hard to catch birds with an empty hand.— *German*

One beats the bush and another catches the bird.

Throwing your cap at a bird is not the best way to catch it.

He will never catch a bird in flight if he cannot keep his own in a cage.— *Persian*

The bird sees the grain but not the snare.

Birds are caught with grain and men with money.—*Armenian*

Old birds are not caught with cats.—*Dutch*

An old bird will not enter a cage.—*Spanish*

Every bird is fond of its own note.—*Welsh*

As the old bird sings, so does the young one.

A bird chooses its tree, the tree the bird.—*Chinese*

Sweet as a cuckoo warbling in a garden are the charming words of the wise, but the words of the bad are as vile as the cawing of a crow.

Wood birds sing in the morning, water birds cry at night.—*Chinese*

If a bird sings too early beware of the cat.—*Russian*

Birds are entangled by their feet, and men by their tongues.

How can a kite know the prey of a hawk?—*Hindi*

He esteems the crow and the nightingale alike.—*Turkish*

Better a bird of the wood than one of the cage.—*German*

Birds of prey do not flock together or sing together—*German*

A man will die for riches just as a bird will die for food.

A crane in a tree soon breaks its leg.—*Finnish*

A crane, frightened at the roar of thunder, fears even a jackal's howl.—*Pashto*

A bird flying into the house brings good luck.—*Japanese*

A man must not spoil the pheasant's tail.—*Italian*

The pigeon never knows woe.

When the snare has been taken up, the pigeons arrive.—*Malay*

Though you may feed a jungle bird out of a gold plate, it will make for the jungle nevertheless.—*Malay*

Silly birds fly first.—*Chinese*

The bird flying in the air does not trouble the water.—*Japanese*

People live like birds together in a wood; when the time comes, each takes flight.—*Chinese*

The guinea hen does not breed in captivity. — *Swahili*

The flying bird gets something; the sitting bird nothing. — *Swedish*

The bird does not feel its wing heavy. — *Turkish*

When the falcon prepares for a swoop, he forgets everything but his present object. — *Pashto*

Though the osprey go high, she does not reach to heaven. — *Swahili*

Birds seek shelter in a bushy tree, men seek aid from the wealthy. — *Bengali*

Butterfly

The butterfly becomes only when it's entirely ready. — *Chinese*

The butterfly often forgets it was a caterpillar.

Fickle as a butterfly. — *Arabic*

Camel

The dexterity of a camel is known when you travel on a narrow bridge. — *Armenian*

If the camel gets his nose in the tent, his body will soon follow. — *Arabic*

If a camel comes to the village of ignorant people, they all declare that their ancestor has risen from the dead.

The camel has his projects, and the camel driver has his projects. — *Arabic*

The load is laid upon the camel according to its strength.

When the camel wants straw, he stretches out his neck. — *Persian*

Chamois leather is not made of a camel's hide.

Death is a black camel that kneels at every man's gate. —*Turkish*

Everything with a crooked neck is not a camel. —*Arabic*

The kick of the camel is soft, but stunning. —*Turkish*

A camel going to seek horns lost its ears. —*Persian*

He who makes himself a camel must not grumble at the burden. —*Arabic*

He who steals an egg will steal a camel. —*Arabic*

Making a fool understand is like making a camel leap a ditch. —*Turkish*

If you love, love a moon, and if you steal, steal a camel. —*Arabic*

There is no telling on which side the camel will lie down.

The camel crouches down on the place of another camel. —*Arabic*

Yoke not a camel and a cat together. —*Persian*

The anger of a camel is unforgiving. —*Greek*

Whoever rushes between two camels is kicked by both. —*Turkish*

There are three things never hidden: love, a mountain and one riding on a camel. —*Arabic*

If the camel could see its hump, it would fall down and break its neck. —*Urdu*

He, like a camel in his might, prefers the heavy to the light. —*Chinese*

Those who keep camels should have high gateways. —*Pashto*

Cat

A cat is called a domestic tiger and the king of rats. —*Tamil*

When the cat is away, the rats dance on the table. —*Swedish*

The cat loves fish but not wet feet.

Biting and scratching got the cat with kitten.

When the lights are out, all cats are gray.

A cat in gloves catches no mice.

He who plays with a cat must bear its scratches. — *Arabic*

Keep no more cats than will catch mice.

By the cat's good luck, the string is broken. — *Hindi*

Though the cat winks a while, she is not blind.

Let the cat wink and let the mouse run.

In a forest of brambles, a cat is a tiger. — *Hindi*

When the master leaves the high seat, up jumps the cat. — *Norwegian*

The cat causes bad dreams to the mouse. — *Armenian*

The dream of the cat is all about the mice. — *Arabic*

Whoever will not feed the cats must feed the mice and the rats. — *German*

The cat is in the dove house. — *Spanish*

The more you stroke a cat's back, the higher she raises her tail. — *Gaelic*

He who laughs too much has the nature of a fool, he who laughs not at all has the nature of an old cat.

To the old cat give a tender mouse. — *Italian*

A cat has nine lives as the onion has seven skins. — *German*

It is too much to expect a cat who sits next to milk not to lap it up. — *German*

Will the cat that has come for new milk drink buttermilk? — *Tamil*

It was the cat's luck that the net broke. — *Hindi*

The cat hates the dog that bites her. — *Welsh*

They trusted the key of the pigeon coop to the cat. — *Arabic*

A fierce cat rules nine households. — *Chinese*

Good greetings soften a cat. — *Russian*

Many big cats do not catch a rat. — *Swahili*

As a cat follows a mouse, so a fool forsakes not his anger. — *Bengali*

Chicken

Even clever hens sometimes lay their eggs among nettles. — *German*

It is not the hen that cackles who lays the most eggs. — *German*

Unlaid eggs are uncertain chickens.

Hens likes to lay in a nest that already has eggs. — *German*

It is not common for hens to have pillows. — *Gaelic*

Although the fox runs, the chicken has wings.

Some people wrangle about an egg but let the hens fly away. — *German*

Children and chickens must always be picking.

A hen's eyes are with her chicks. — *French*

Prepare a nest for a hen and she will lay eggs for you. — *Portuguese*

A hen will not complain for the hawk's being sick. — *Welsh*

The hen scratches and the chickens learn. — *Kashmiri*

Chickens do not die from the hen's kick. — *Kashmiri*

A chicken raised with the pig will eat dirt. — *Tamil*

By appearance an eagle, but by intelligence a black rooster. — *Russian*

It is a sad house where the hen crows louder than the rooster. — *Italian*

As the old rooster crows, so does the young. — *German*

All roosters must have a comb. — *Dutch*

The fool is a rooster who sings at the wrong time. — *Turkish*

In cold weather, roosters crow at midnight. — *Chinese*

Young roosters love no coops.

The rooster shuts his eyes when he crows because he knows it by heart. — *German*

A good rooster crows in any hen house.

The hen lives by picks as the lion by prey. — *Danish*

It is natural for a rooster to proclaim. — *Welsh*

Those who eat eggs don't know what the chicken suffered.

The chicken knows the serpent's sneezing. — *Bengali*

The hen that stays at home picks up the crumbs. — *Portuguese*

In your own village, cock and crow, but in another, you must be a hen. — *Bengali*

Clouds

Though the cloud be black, white water falls from it.

A rich miser is a summer cloud without the rain. — *Arabic*

When the floating clouds are dispersed, we see a clear sky.— *Chinese*

Opportunities pass away like clouds.— *Arabic*

The higher the clouds, the finer the weather.

A learned man without practice is like a cloud without water.— *Arabic*

After clouds comes clear weather.— *Danish*

The clouds that thunder do not always bring rain.— *Armenian*

Clouds would have appeared if it was going to rain.— *Arabic*

Cloudy mornings turn into clear evenings.— *Italian*

A small cloud may hide both sun and moon.— *German*

Clouds that the sun builds up, darken it.

As clouds frequently obscure the sun, so do the passions obscure the reasoning power.

One cloud is enough to eclipse all the sun.

A black cloud threatens, but a white cloud gives rain.

When the clouds appear like rocks and towers, the earth is refreshed by frequent showers.

Storms in the conscience will always put clouds on your face.

Mount the clouds and ride the mist as Buddhas and fairies do.— *Chinese*

Clouds pass, but the rains remain.— *Chinese*

If there were no clouds, we should not enjoy the sun.

There is no sun so bright that clouds will not overcast it.— *Scottish*

The world's unfavorable views of behavior and character are but as the floating clouds from which the brightest day is not free.— *Chinese*

Cow

For the reason that cows nourish all men and give them happiness is the very reason why people should love and honor them.—*Burmese*

I cannot sell the cow and have the milk.—*Scottish*

The cow that moves about will find pasture.—*Hindi*

The cow knows not the value of her tail until she has lost it.

Even a holy cow, if found with a stolen one, may be impounded.—*Bengali*

Many a good cow has a bad calf.

The cow licks no strange calf.—*German*

Faraway cows have long horns.

A cow is not called dapper unless she has a spot.—*Danish*

As a calf, though put among a thousand cows, finds its mother, so a deed, though done in the time gone by, flies to the doer.—*Hindi*

A mad bull is not to be tied up with a pack thread.

It's hard to take a horn off a hornless cow.—*Gaelic*

All is not butter that comes from a cow.

Although the cow is black, it's milk is white.—*Pashto*

The best of all animals is the cow.—*Welsh*

A cow never goes so far that its tail does not follow.—*Norwegian*

Crab

It is because of his good heart that a crab has no head.

The greatest crabs do not always have the best meat.

You can never make a crab go in a straight direction. — *Persian*

A crab tells its young ones to go straight. — *Malay*

When fish are few, a crab will do. — *Polish*

When the crab lifts its claw, the matter has come to pass long since. — *Swahili*

Crocodile

A crocodile in the water can destroy an elephant; out of the stream, it is discomforted even by a dog. Where the skillful is not at home, he is of no avail. — *Hindi*

The stubborn and crocodiles are alike; they will not lose hold of what they have seized. — *Tamil*

Two crocodiles do not live in one hole.

Live in the river and fight the crocodiles. — *Hindi*

When water is still do not imagine there are no crocodiles. — *Malay*

Crow

A flying crow always catches something. — *German*

If you put a crow in a cage will it talk like a parrot? — *Urdu*

A crow satisfies his passions in secret, is very cautions, eats food in company with his relatives, is observant and industrious; these are the five acts of a crow. — *Burmese*

A crow is never whiter for washing itself often.

You may wash the crow with rosewater but it's feathers won't become white. — *Malay*

Will a crow become a swan by bathing in the Ganges? — *Tamil*

The crow does not roost with the phoenix. — *Chinese*

Old crows are hard to catch.—*German*

Like a group of crows, it begins with a "caw" and ends with a "caw".—*Arabic*

The crow in imitating the swan's gait forgot its own.—*Hindi*

Among a hundred crows what can one cuckoo do?

Crows are black all the world over.—*Chinese*

The cry of the old crow is made by the little crow.—*Welsh*

Away from our native country even a crow is dear.—*Russian*

There never was so bad a crow that it did not want a mate.—*Norwegian*

Day

Another day, like that which is passing, will not come again.—*Arabic*

Daylight will peep through a small hole.—*Scottish*

It is not in the morning that a fine day is to be praised.

One day is as good as two to him who does everything in its place.—*French*

Days go, but spoken words remain.—*Bengali*

The day is short and there is much work to be done in it. A chance day is better than a chosen one.—*Chinese*

The day blots out the dread of night.—*Arabic*

What is wrong today will not be right tomorrow.—*Dutch*

The better the day, the better the deed.—*Spanish*

He that thinks in his bed has a day without a night.

A man cannot become perfect in a hundred years, but he may become corrupt in less than a day.—*Chinese*

As the day lengthens, the cold strengthens.—*Scottish*

Today secures not tomorrow's affairs. —*Chinese*

Have you ever seen a day which ends not in the evening? —*Turkish*

Make the night night, and the day day, and you will be merry and wise.

Every day is a leaf in your history.

The longest day must have an end.

Deer

Lofty is the deer's head on the summit of the mountains. —*Gaelic*

What matters if the deer has more or fewer spots? —*Tamil*

An army of stags is more to be feared under the command of a lion, than an army of lions led by a stag.

In peace they are lions, in the battle deer.

The fawn's speed is hereditary. —*Gaelic*

Will the spots of a deer vanish by jumping from one jungle to another? —*Sinhalese*

A salmon from the pool, a wand from the wood, and a deer from the hills are thefts which no man can be ashamed to own. —*Gaelic*

The mouse-deer may forget the net, but the net won't forget the mouse-deer. —*Malay*

The stag and the tiger do not stroll together. —*Chinese*

The older the buck gets, the harder his horns get. —*Swedish*

The deer chained with a golden chain, if he escapes, hastens to the forest to eat grass. —*Malay*

Dog

Even the street dog has his lucky days. —*Japanese*

Every dog has his day, and every man his hour.

A grateful dog is better than a thankless man.

Beware of a silent dog and still water.

A jackal gives luck to those he meets but let him beware of a dog. —*Hindi*

Dogs have teeth in all countries. —*German*

The dog guards the night, the cock rules the morning. —*Chinese*

The dog bites not his master.

Great barkers are not biters. —*Scottish*

Dogs bark as they are bred.

An old dog cannot change his way of barking.

The dog in his kennel barks at his fleas, but the dog who is hunting does not feel them.

All aren't thieves that dogs bark at.

Chase a dog down a passage and he will turn again and bite you. —*Chinese*

A man may cause his own dog to bite him.

Barking dogs seldom bite.

Dogs that bark at a distance never bite.

If the old dog barks, he gives counsel. —*Italian*

An old dog does not bark for nothing. —*German*

The dog barks more out of habit than care of the house.

One dog barks at something and a hundred bark at him. —*Chinese*

Dogs bark and the wind carries it away. —*Russian*

First the big dog barks, then the little one. —*Pashto*

Love me, love my dog. —*French*

A dog knows how he manages to eat bones.

A dog with a bone knows no friend. —*German*

Two dogs strive for a bone and the third runs away with it.

Two dogs and a bone never agree. —*Persian*

A good dog deserves a good bone.

A good dog never barks about a bone. —*Scottish*

Dogs are generally fond of bones, and people of their relatives. —*Bengali*

Into the mouth of a bad dog often falls a good bone. —*French*

A dog at hand is better than a brother far off.

Hunting dogs have scratched faces.

It is a good dog that can catch anything.

A good dog hunts by instinct. —*German*

Only the silly dog chases the flying bird. —*Chinese*

A living dog is better than a dead lion.

The dog is boldest at home. —*Norwegian*

The dog has four paws, but it is not able to go four different ways.

A dog seeing a dog shows its teeth to harm, a bad man being irritable on seeing a good man wishes to oppress him. —*Burmese*

It is not good to wake a sleeping dog or a lion.—*Italian*

A dog is not idle, is easily content, sleeps easily and rises easily, is a staunch attendant and full of bravery; these are six attributes of a dog.—*Burmese*

When the dog is awake, the shepherd may sleep.—*German*

He who lies down with dogs must rise up with fleas.—*Spanish*

The dog is loud-mouthed in the house of its master.

Every dog is valiant at his own door.

Dogs that fight each other will unite against the wolf.—*Armenian*

The dog does not bite the ear of another dog.—*Arabic*

If you make a dog a king, will he not still gnaw leather?—*Hindi*

Where there are dogs, there are arguments.—*Tamil*

Quarrelsome dogs get dirty coats.—*German*

A mischievous cur must be tied short.—*French*

Quarreling dogs come halting home.

The dog presumes on his master's power.—*Chinese*

A dog knows his own master.—*Turkish*

The dog understands his master's mood.—*Chinese*

The most careless is a servant, the one most faithful is a dog.—*Welsh*

The dog has no aversion to a poor family.—*Chinese*

If you kiss a dog, it licks your whole face.—*Telugu*

Dogs have more good in them than men think they have.—*Chinese*

In a great house even the dog is respected. —*Hindi*

A dog is a dog whatever his color. —*German*

Dogs will go to a corner that's open. — *Gaelic*

A modest dog seldom grows fat. —*German*

Even a dog remembers old favors. —*Russian*

If you wish the dog to follow you, feed him.

The cat steals the rice and the dog comes and eats it. —*Chinese*

The dog that goes to many weddings eats in none from wishing to eat at all of them. —*Spanish*

The coat of a grinning dog is covered with flavor. —*Welsh*

Even the dog gets bread by wagging its tail. —*German*

It's the nature of a greyhound to be long-tailed. —*Spanish*

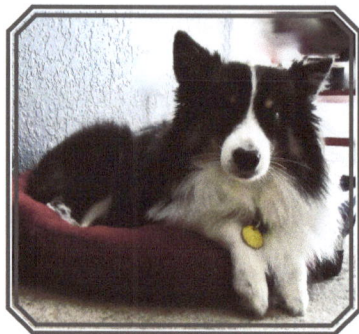

A dog's tail never stands straight. —*Arabic*

Do not step on a dog's tail. —*Hindi*

If a dog bites, do not bite back. —*Thai*

One cannot throw stones every time a dog barks, neither can one follow the advice of everyone. —*Bengali*

A stupid dog is not a tiger. —*Russian*

Better a dog's love than his hatred. —*Welsh*

Nothing so fierce as a dog. —*Welsh*

The dog that is idle is never tired of running. —*Turkish*

A dog is disliked for his teeth, a man for this tongue. —*Bengali*

He who has a dog need not bark himself. —*Norwegian*

Donkey

An ass covered with gold is more respected than a horse with a pack saddle.

He who mounts an ass has one shame, but he who falls from it has two. —*Armenian*

Better ride on an ass that carries me than a horse that throws me. —*Spanish*

Every ass thinks himself worthy to stand with the king's horse.

In the time of need we even call a donkey a king. —*Hindi*

The ass that carries wine drinks water.

An ass that carries a load is better than a lion that devours men.

The ass that brays eats the most.

A donkey's tail is not a horse's tail.

An ass is the gravest beast, an owl the gravest bird.

He that makes himself an ass must not take it bad if men ride him.

If an ass goes traveling, he will not come home a horse.

Even an ass will not fall twice in the same quicksand.

Every ass loves to hear himself bray.

Joke with an ass and he will flap you in he face with his tail.

Fear makes the ass run more rapidly than the horse. —*Armenian*

A sleeping ass eats no barley. —*Persian*

Repetition will teach the donkey. —*Arabic*

When someone gives you a donkey, you must not examine the bridle.

When the donkey has eaten, he scatters his fodder. —*Arabic*

Duck

Young ducks are all swimmers.— *Arabic*

What is good for the goose is good for the duck.

Duck's eggs are bigger than hen's eggs.

When the goose won't have it, it is given to the duck.— *Malay*

Proud are ducks in the rain.— *Welsh*

When you travel by boat be prepared for a duck.— *Chinese*

Eagle

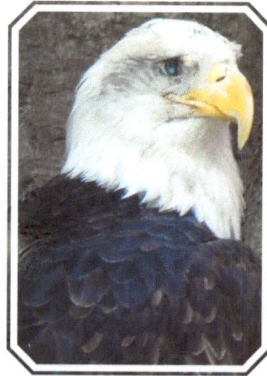

As the scream of the eagle is heard when she has passed over, so a man's name remains after his death.— *Chinese*

The old age of an eagle is as good as the youth of a sparrow.— *Greek*

Eagles do not breed doves.— *German*

Eagles fly alone but sheep flock together.— *German*

An eagle does not hunt flies.— *French*

The eagle does not war against frogs.— *Italian*

The strength of an eagle is in his beak.— *Welsh*

The dog chases out the quail, but the eagle claims it.— *Japanese*

The eagle soars alone.

Where there are no eagles, the grasshoppers will say, "We are eagles." — *Malay*

The eagle loves the mountain.

Elephant

To an elephant you must give a berth 1,000 feet wide, to a horse 100, to horned creatures 10, but to keep clear of a bad person, you must leave the area.

Only an elephant can carry an elephant's load.

The footprints of all animals are included in an elephant's.

An elephant has one set of teeth for eating and another for show.

An elephant, however lean, is valuable.

Greater than the camel is the elephant.—*Turkish*

If there were no elephant in the jungle, the buffalo would be large.

In a bad place even the foot of an elephant slips.

An elephant is not frightened by a barking dog.—*Hindi*

An elephant fears not fish, neither do the good fear the bad.

Never despise your enemy because he is weak; an ant can kill an elephant by entering its trunk.—*Hindi*

Keep out of the elephant's path.—*Thai*

With one hair of a woman you can tether even a great elephant.—*Japanese*

The doctor can be deceived as much as the four-footed elephant can take a false step.—*Thai*

It is possible to stop an elephant with a kick; for everything there is a remedy, but no cure for the headstrong.

The soul excited by anger is like furious elephants breaking the cords with which they are bound.

An elephant is an elephant whether on high ground or low.

When two elephants jostle, the one who gets hurt is the grass.—*Swahili*

After an elephant's tusks are grown, he cannot ungrow them; what a person has once spat forth is not again returned into the mouth.—*Bengali*

Fish

A fish appears larger in the water than it really is.—*Armenian*

Don't teach fish to swim. —*German*

The best fish swim near the bottom.

It is ill angling after the net.

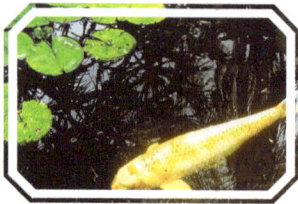

Fish and guests smell at three days old.

Fish follow the bait.

An unlucky fish takes bad bait. —*Scottish*

Fish are not to be caught with a birdcall.

The fish will soon be caught that nibbles at every bait.

All fish are not caught with flies.

An unhappy fish often gets unhappy bait.

When whales fight, even shrimps' backs are broken. —*Korean*

There are as good fish in the sea as ever were caught.

Use a small fish to catch a great one.

The little fish splashes even in a mouthful of water.

It is useless to cast nets into a river where there are no fish. —*Spanish*

Better go home and make a net than go down the river and desire to get fish. —*Chinese*

Great fish break the net. —*German*

The fish who seeks the fish hook sees his ruin. —*Spanish*

Man sees the gain not the danger, just as the fish sees the bait and not the hook. —*Chinese*

A fish comes to his senses after he gets into the net. —*Turkish*

Small fish are better than none. —*Scottish*

The fish that escapes is a big one. —*Turkish*

It is the bait that lures, not the fisherman or the rod. —*German*

In shallow water the fish appears. —*Chinese*

It's easy to catch fish in troubled water. —*Armenian*

When you paddle up the canal and make the water muddy, you will catch fish. —*Chinese*

Fish see and understand each other in the water. —*Pashto*

It is good fishing in troubled waters.

Are minnows found at every fair? —*Korean*

Wherever there is water there are fish. —*Malay*

He who would catch fish must not mind getting wet. —*Persian*

Let every herring hang by its own tail. —*Gaelic*

There is no fishing for trout in dry pants. —*Spanish*

Big fish eat the small ones. —*Russian*

If a bridge falls it won't crush the minnows. —*Chinese*

You cannot hide an eel in a sack.

Fish help water, water helps fish. —*Chinese*

A prawn is not accepted among fish; a poor man is not counted among the rich. —*Bengali*

Flowers

Every flower has its perfume. —*Turkish*

A cottager's garden can also bear flowers. —*Norwegian*

The fallen blossom never returns to the branch. —*Japanese*

Every flower has its perfume, every age its needs. —*Armenian*

The fragrance of the flower is never borne against the breeze, but the fragrance of human virtues diffuses itself everywhere. —*Hindi*

Fair flowers do not remain long by the wayside. —*German*

One flower does not make a garland.

He makes believe that his gourd flower is a hyacinth. —*Korean*

Not every flower smells sweet. —*German*

April showers bring forth May flowers.

The flower is worn in the ear but the stalk is cast aside. —*Malay*

Painted flowers have no scent. —*German*

The flowers will blossom again, but youth is not perennial. —*Chinese*

Plant flowers with care and they may never grow; stick willows in carelessly and they may yield a pleasant shade.

Vanity is a flower that never comes to fruition. —*Spanish*

As the cherry flower is the first among flowers, so should the warrior be first among men. —*Japanese*

The peony is merely beautiful to look at; the date, though it has a small flower bears a good fruit. —*Chinese*

If you want to enjoy the fruit, do not pluck the flower. —*German*

Peaches blossom in the second month; chrysanthemums in the ninth are out; each must wait till its time comes about. —*Chinese*

Good qualities, though hidden, become unveiled and shine throughout the world. The flower of the jasmine although dried up, sends a sweet fragrance everywhere. —*Tibetan*

From the same flower the serpent draws its poison and the bee its honey. —*Armenian*

A meager soil produces late flowers; a poor man acquires wealth but slowly. —*Chinese*

She is a flower without fragrance. —*Persian*

If you smell a flower too long, you lose the scent; if you eat too much, you lose the flavor. —*Bengali*

The begonia is the immortal among flowers. —*Chinese*

As in the flower, the fragrance, in the sesame seed the oil, in wood the fire, in milk the butter, and in the cane the sugar—so guard with your best mind the soul in the body. —*Hindi*

The hibiscus opens in the morning and droops at night. —*Chinese*

Though the oleander has a flower like a rose, it doesn't become a rose. —*Pashto*

As flowers send their perfume on the breeze, so does news travel from person to person. —*Bengali*

Fly

A fly is nothing yet it creates loathsomeness. —*Arabic*

Laws catch flies, but let hornets go free.

Every fly has its shadow. —*German*

Flies don't land on a boiling pot.

Even a fly has its anger. —*German*

Flies find the wounds, bees the flowers; good men the worthwhile, common men the faults. —*Hindi*

A live fly cannot be swallowed.

The fly knows the face of the milk seller. —*Arabic*

Haste is only good for catching flies. —*Russian*

Big flies break the spider's web. —*German*

Although the fly be small among insects, it has the power to turn the stomach of a man. —*Turkish*

Fiddlers, dogs and flies come to feasts uncalled. —*Scottish*

Fox

The brains of a fox will be of little service if you play with the paw of a lion.

The fox is very cunning, but whoever catches him more cunning. — *Spanish*

The fox knows much, but more is he who catches him.

A fox should not be on the jury at a goose's trial.

The fox was asked: "Who is your witness?" — "My tail," he answered. — *Armenian*

It is a silly goose that comes to a fox's sermon.

When the fox wants to catch geese, he wags his tail. — *German*

It's bad to give the fox the geese to keep.

The fox may grow gray but never good.

If you want to catch a fox, you must hunt with geese. — *Danish*

When the fox licks his paw, let the farmer look after his geese. — *Danish*

Whoever is the fox's servant must carry his tail. — *Gaelic*

With foxes, you must play the fox. — *Persian*

The fox has 100 proverbs to tell about 99 fowls. — *Turkish*

Foxes, when they cannot reach the grapes, say they are not there.

The fox preys farthest from his hole.

Foxes dig not their own holes.

A good fox has three holes. — *Russian*

An old fox understands a trap.

An old fox does not go twice into the trap. — *German*

Old foxes need no tutors.

It is a poor fox that has only one hole. — *German*

The sleeping fox catches no poultry.

Poverty is cunning, it catches even a fox. —*German*

When the fox is hungry, he pretends that he is asleep. —*Greek*

When the fox is asleep nothing falls into his mouth. —*French*

The fox sits but once on the thorns. —*Armenian*

The fox has only one wish. Not to see the dog and not be seen by him. —*Armenian*

If you go hunting fox be prepared to meet a lion. —*Hindi*

The fox knows well where the geese dwell. —*Welsh*

The fox thought his own shadow very large. —*Urdu*

For lack of hens, the fox catches crows. —*Swedish*

Frog

A frog in a well sees nothing of the great ocean. —*Japanese*

A frog in a well can hardly get out. —*Chinese*

He who does not go forth and explore all the earth is a well frog.

The well frog is best in the well. —*Chinese*

One of little knowledge being presumptuous thinks that little is a great deal; a frog not seeing the water in the sea thinks the water in a well is considerable. —*Burmese*

The toad, living near the lotus, tastes not its honey; the illiterate, living near the learned, remain ignorant. —*Hindi*

The frog mounted on a clod said he had seen Kashmir.

Set a frog on a golden stool, off it goes again into the pool. —*German*

Gossips and frogs drink and talk.

Where the frogs are croaking it is there that silence is appreciated.

The cuckoo does well to relapse into stillness with the incoming rainy season. When the frogs are chirping, silence is most befitting. —*Hindi*

When the rain is coming, the bullfrogs sing.

The frog sings even though it has no hair or cloth. —*Spanish*

The frog does not bite because it cannot. —*Italian*

The hasty hand catches frogs instead of fish.

It's the frog's own tongue that betrays him.

He is a toad in the well. —*Korean*

The cuckoo drinks celestial juice of the mango tree and is not proud. The frog drinks swamp water and quacks with conceit. —*Hindi*

Dress a little toad in fine clothing and it will look pretty. —*Spanish*

A bad man has a bad man to crush him; the stinging caterpillar has a toad to catch him. —*Chinese*

The body of a frog, but the voice of an ox. Small men are often the best workers. — *Bengali*

Goat

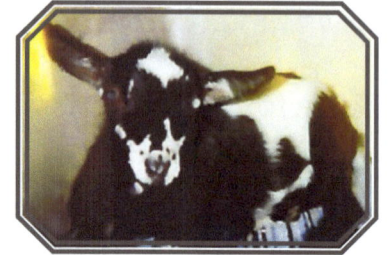

A goat is not easy to fence in. — *Norwegian*

The foolish goat eats at the foot of the hill.

The goat who climbs up the rocks must climb down again. —*French*

An old goat is never the more revered for his beard.

Where the goat leaps, the kid will follow. —*Spanish*

It is not easy to gather wool from a goat. —*Welsh*

Once scabby goat infects the flock. —*Persian*

The goat who isn't cunning never gets fat.

If you don't mind bother, buy a goat.—*Pashto*

The goat's business is not the sheep's affair.

The wretched goat makes the herdsman wretched.—*Swahili*

If a beard were all, the goat would be the winner.—*Danish*

Where the goat is tied, she must browse.—*French*

Goose

A goose, gander and gosling have three sounds but are one thing.

When one goose drinks, all drink.—*German*

A wild goose never laid a tame egg.—*Gaelic*

The wild goose brings the beginning of autumn.—*Chinese*

You must walk a long while behind a wild goose before you will find an ostrich feather.—*Danish*

If all fools wore white caps, we should look like a flock of geese.

The goose hisses, but does not bite.—*Dutch*

The goose with a good gander cackles loudly.—*German*

The goslings will lead the geese out to grass.—*French*

The goose and the paddy bird are of one color and frolic in the same pool. The goose extracts the milk from the water and the paddy bird drinks the mire.—*Hindi*

A goose drinks as much as a gander.—*German*

Every man thinks his own geese to be swans.

To give advice to a fool is like throwing water on a goose.—*Danish*

A goose, frequently while looking for clusters of lotuses and not seeing well in the night, is deceived by the image of the star in the water, and does not try to pluck the water lily even in the day for fear it may only be another reflection. People, who have been made timid often through deception, fear danger even when among good people.—*Hindi*

Watch out for the geese when the fox preaches.

Just as there is no place to where the wild goose cannot flap its wings in flight, there are no lengths that a man attracted by gain and fame will not go.—*Chinese*

The gray goose will be caught last.—*German*

It is of no use making shoes for geese.—*Danish*

One goose generally follows another.

A goose quill is more dangerous than a lion's claw.

It is the nature of the wild goose to follow the brightness, thus it is called the bird of the bright element.—*Chinese*

There is many a goose besides the one that has feathers.—*Welsh*

Grass

Every blade of grass has its share of the dews of heaven.—*Chinese*

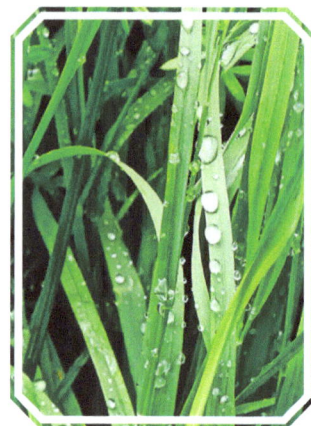

The sweeter the grass, the nearer the earth.—*Welsh*

Grass at a distance looks thick.—*Bengali*

No grass grows on a worn road.—*German*

If the fields could talk, we should know too many secrets.

Grass grows not under a stone.—*Kurdish*

Even a blade of grass is a weapon to the strong.—*Tamil*

Bad grass does not make good hay. —*German*

Just as the grass dreads severe frost and the frost dreads the sun, so does one wicked man dread the oppression of others more wicked than himself. —*Chinese*

If the root remains, the grass will grow. —*Chinese*

The steed will live who nibbles the grass of May. —*Welsh*

Three things increase in rain—grass, thistles and eider (ducks). —*Welsh*

Hare

The very falling of leaves frightens hares.

Running hares do not need the spur. —*Italian*

Many hounds may soon worry a hare.

Hares are not caught with drums. —*German*

As mad as a March hare.

The hare catches the lion in a net of gold. —*Italian*

If you run after two hares, you will catch neither.

Who hunts two hares, leaves one and loses the other. —*Italian*

When we least expect it, the hare darts out of the ditch. —*Dutch*

Hawk

All birds cannot be hawks. —*Norwegian*

The hawk is not frightened by the cries of a crane. —*Arabic*

It is hard to lure hawks with empty hands. —*Danish*

The talented hawk hides its claws.

The hawk, though hungry, will not peck at grain.—*Japanese*

He who makes himself a dove is eaten by the hawk.—*Italian*

You cannot make a hawk out of a buzzard.—*French*

It's easier to make a hawk of a kite than to make a learned man of a bumpkin.—*Welsh*

Never a hawk flies so high it will not fall to some lure.—*Scottish*

Heron

One heron among a hundred crows is a prince.

To an overfed heron, all fish are bad.—*Hindi*

The heron is a saint as long as the fish is not in sight.—*Bengali*

When the heron and oyster quarreled, the fisherman got the benefit.—*Chinese*

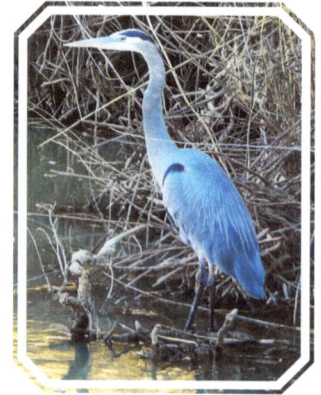

The heron blames the water because he cannot swim.—*Danish*

However high the heron flies, at last he lands on the buffalo's rump.—*Malay*

Hill

Hills see, walls hear.—*Spanish*

It is difficult to roll a stone to the top of a hill.—*Tamil*

No one runs open-mouthed up a hill; do not run headlong into anger.—*Bengali*

Following virtue is like ascending a hill, following vice is like rushing down a mountain.—*Chinese*

It is difficult to climb a steep hill, but 10 times more difficult to teach a fool.—*Bengali*

Huge winds blow on high hills.

Do not speak of secret matters in a field that is full of little hills.

Every hill has its valley.—*German*

He who stays in the valley will never get over the hill.—*French*

Horse

A fast horse doesn't need a spur.—*German*

It is easy to go on foot if you lead your horse by the bridle.—*French*

A straw rope is the bridle for a stray horse.—*Tamil*

Look not a gift horse in the mouth.—*French*

Distance reveals the strength of a horse, time, the character of a man. —*Chinese*

The biggest horses are not the best travelers.

A big horse is not frisky.—*Hindi*

The horse thinks one thing and its rider another.

Trust not a horse's heel nor a dog's tooth.

You cannot tell a piebald horse until you see him.—*Gaelic*

Do horns grow on a horse's head?—*Korean*

You may know a horse by his harness.

Better to lose the saddle than the horse.—*German*

A horse cannot be judged by its saddle.

Either win the horse or lose the saddle.

Always put the saddle on the right horse.

Who eats his dinner alone must saddle his horse alone. — *Spanish*

Just as one horse does not carry two saddles so a loyal statesman will not serve two masters. — *Chinese*

A horse is neither better nor worse for his trappings.

The best horse needs breaking, and the smartest child needs teaching.

The gray mare is the better horse.

A mare without her rider finds the meadow. — *Spanish*

An old mare's foal is known in a herd. — *Gaelic*

A colt is worth noting if it does not break its halter. — *French*

Mend the stable after the horse has left. — *Korean*

Never let go the reins of the wild colt in your heart. — *Japanese*

A wild colt may become a good horse.

Many a dark horse has a bright future.

You may break a colt, but not an old horse.

Ride a horse and a mare on the shoulders, an ass and a mule on the rear. — *Spanish*

A generation is like a swift horse passing a crevice. — *Chinese*

A short halter for a greedy horse. — *German*

A good horse has no need of the spur. — *Italian*

A good horse cannot be of a bad color.

A good horse resembles a superior man.

Let a horse drink when he will, but not what he will.

A hungry horse makes a clean manger. —*Spanish*

The horse opens its mouth when you say oats, shuts it when you say bridle. —*Tamil*

A bad horse eats as much as a good one. —*German*

It is easy to catch a blind horse. —*Welsh*

Better a poor horse than an empty stall. —*German*

Where the horse lies down, some hair will be found.

Every horse thinks its pack is heaviest.

The kick of a quiet horse strikes strong. —*Armenian*

The horse knows its owner.

The horse never turns its back on its master.

Misfortunes come on horseback and go away on foot. —*French*

If you get from a man an ox, return to him a horse. —*Chinese*

When two ride a horse, one must be behind. —*Hindi*

Touch a galled horse and he'll kick.

A horse that does not stumble is the best horse. —*Tamil*

A horse may run fast, but it cannot run away from its tail. —*Russian*

When riding a white horse with bright new red trappings, you will have a relationship thrust upon you by even those who are unrelated to you. But if one morning your horse is dead and your gold is gone, your relatives and acquaintances will treat you just the same as the man in the street. —*Chinese*

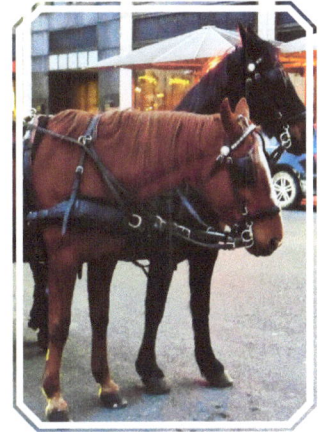

A quiet man is taken advantage of and a quiet horse is ridden by everyone.—*Chinese*

With Latin, a horse and money, you will pass through the world.—*Spanish*

Even a good horse stumbles.—*Russian*

A good horse sometimes stumbles; the tongue of a good person sometimes trips.—*Bengali*

The horse can stand the horse's kick.—*Pashto*

It is too late to lock the stable door when the steed is stolen.—*German*

A valuable horse is kept in the stable and a good doctor always finds employment in the sick room.—*Bengali*

Ragged colts make the handsomest stallions.—*German*

By a long journey we learn a horse's strength, the length of days shows a person's heart.—*Chinese*

The losing horse blames its saddle.—*German*

Where one horse won't go, a hundred fear to step.—*Chinese*

Four horses cannot overtake a tongue. —*Chinese*

A horse eats his earnings.

Insects

Does a dragonfly have eyebrows?—*Korean*

Insects of every kind covet life and fear death.—*Chinese*

The fatter the flea, the leaner the dog. —*German*

The cockroach is never silly enough to approach the door of the hen house.

The mosquito is little, but when it sings, your ears are filled with its sound.

The mosquito wastes time when it tries to sting the alligator.

Will lice attach themselves to a bald head?—*Tamil*

A centipede does not become lame by breaking one leg.—*Hindi*

When a centipede dies, it does not fall prostrate because its supporters are many.—*Chinese*

Why pull down the house for fear of bugs?—*Tamil*

The cricket's life—hungry all day and at night noisy.—*Spanish*

A man is a dragon with money in the store; he's an insect without it, and nothing more.—*Chinese*

Wherever there is field, there will be grasshoppers.—*Malay*

A grasshopper opening its eyes is not so bad as a leopard clenching his paw.—*Swahili*

Jackal

A jackal's intellect is great.

As a jackal brands itself in imitation of the stripes of a tiger.—*Tamil*

When hunting a jackal take weapons used in hunting a tiger. —*Hindi*

It is said that the jackal of the palm grove cheated the city fox.—*Tamil*

A jackal is pleased with drizzling rain.

If the jackal becomes fat, it will not remain in its hole.—*Tamil*

The jackal prowls all night in search of prey.—*Arabic*

The howling of the jackal will reach the ocean.—*Tamil*

The slyness of a jackal and courage of a tiger.

The jackal's messenger is a jackal, the lion's is a lion.—*Pashto*

All jackals do not have horns.

The jackal's evil fate drives him toward the village.

Like death to oppress a poor person, but like a jackal to run from a strong and influential one.

The dog is the jackal's brother. —*Arabic*

Be at enmity with a jackal, collect an army of tigers. —*Pashto*

Lark

It is better to hear the lark sing, than the mouse chirp.

If the sky were to fall, we'd catch plenty of larks. —*French*

Go to bed with the lamb, rise with the lark.

Leaf

The fall of a leaf is a whisper to the living. —*Russian*

A tree is known by its fruit, not by its leaves.

Whoever is afraid of leaves must not come into the woods. —*Russian*

No matter how tall a tree grows, its leaves will always fall down to return to its roots. —*Chinese*

Though the tree may be beautiful, it is supported by its green leaves.

The silver maple leaf shows the lining of its leaf before a storm.

When one leaf moves, all the branches shake. —*Chinese*

As water runs off the leaf, so good advice slides off a fool.

There are many leaves on a fig tree, but few real fruit. —*Greek*

Good repute is like the cypress; once cut off, it never gives out a leaf again.—*Italian*

Our time runs like on a stream: first fall the leaves, then the tree.—*Dutch*

The more buds, the more leaves.—*Malay*

Lion

You may know a lion by his claw.—*Gaelic*

To the lion belongs whatever his paw has taken.—*Arabic*

It's not good to wake a sleeping lion.

Have in life the force of a lion, the sagacity of an elephant and the sweetness of the lamb.—*Turkish*

A man is a lion in his own cause.—*Scottish*

Every man has in his heart a lion that sleeps.—*Armenian*

A lion at chase and a lamb at home.

A lion may be indebted to a mouse.

The lion is not so fierce as his picture.—*Italian*

The lion is bold until gray.—*Welsh*

Despise not the weak, the gnat stings the eyes of a lion.

Better to be the tail of a lion than the head of a fox.

The fox's wiles will never enter into a lion's head.

The lion pays no attention to flea bites.—*Swedish*

Even the lion must defend itself against flies.—*German*

A lion does not eat the dog's leftovers.—*Persian*

He eats like a lion, but works like a goat.—*Hindi*

It is more useful to fly from yourself than from a lion.—*Arabic*

Lizard

If the lizard was good to eat, it would never be found under a tub.

The lizard is wide as the snake is long. —*Hindi*

He who has been bitten by a serpent is afraid of a lizard. —*Italian*

The rat eats the cane; the innocent lizard dies for it.

Even the lizard gives the fly time to pray. —*Malay*

The footless lizard is from the same den as the snake. —*Chinese*

In words a tiger, in fighting a lizard. —*Bengali*

The lizard, through the bad luck of having feet, was expelled from the snake tribe. —*Pashto*

Lotus

The lotus is the prince of flowers. —*Chinese*

Life is quivering like a drop of water on a lotus leaf.

The lotus is beautiful, but the beauty of whole flower pot depends on the green leaves encircling it. —*Chinese*

The sun sees many lotuses, but the lotuses only one sun. —*Hindi*

The soul floats like the lotus on the lake, unmoved by the tide.

A face shaped like the petals of the lotus, a voice as pleasing as sandalwood, a heart like a pair of scissors and excessive humility —these are the signs of a bad person.

Worldly possessions are like a drop of water on a lotus leaf.

If you are born in a poor man's hovel, but have wisdom, then you shall be like the lotus flower growing out of the mud.—*Japanese*

A man who misses his chance and a monkey who misses his branch cannot be saved.—*Hindi*

He behaves as a monkey in a house.—*Tamil*

There are no monkeys who will not eat plantain fruit.—*Tamil*

Monkey

Even monkeys fall from trees.—*Japanese*

The monkey laughs when the snail dances.

A monkey never watches his own tail, he watches his neighbor's.

When the monkey reigns, dance before him.—*Arabic*

You cannot teach an old monkey how to make faces.

When an ass is among monkeys, they all make faces at him.—*Spanish*

To instigate a villain to do wrong is like teaching a monkey to climb trees.—*Chinese*

Even in the darkness of the rainy season, a monkey will miss the branch when leaping.—*Tamil*

The monkey dances and skips, but the acrobat gets the presents.—*Hindi*

When young monkeys get hold of flowers, do they not use them?—*Malay*

What could not the lion do if he were a monkey?—*Chinese*

When the tree falls, the monkeys flee.—*Chinese*

Years turn hills into valleys, age makes men into monkeys.—*Bengali*

The old monkey gets the apple.—*French*

Moon

All the world can see the moon in the sky.—*Hindi*

The moon is not seen when the sun shines.

When the moon appears, the darkness flies.—*Hindi*

The full moon does not long remain round, and the bright cloud soon vanishes.—*Chinese*

Great cities have great moons.—*Hindi*

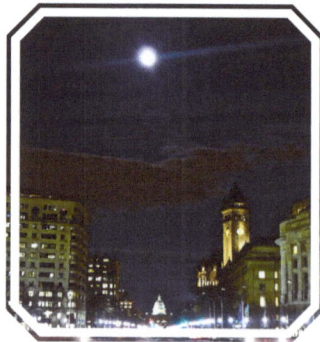

The moon does not grow full in a day.

The full moon does not last and the bright cloud soon vanishes.—*Chinese*

Life is like the moon: now dark, now full.—*Polish*

A halo round the moon is a sign of wind.—*Chinese*

If a circle forms around the moon, it will rain or snow soon.

The moon is not always round; the clouds sometimes disappear.—*Chinese*

Nothing so cold as the moon.—*Welsh*

The year fears mid-autumn as the month the full moon.—*Chinese*

Seek truth from thought, not in moldy books. Look in the sky to find the moon, not in the pool.—*Persian*

The mood of mid-autumn is exceedingly bright.—*Chinese*

Words of blame from those who are hostile to a great man cannot injure him. The moon is not hurt when barked at by a dog.—*Arabic*

The sky full of stars depends on one moon.—*Chinese*

Be graceful as the moon.—*Tamil*

There is moonlight for a few days and the night is as dark as before.

Everyone sees the moon in rising.

A thief's face is like the moon. — *Hindi*

The moon mocks thieves. — *Bengali*

Great men have great troubles, which little men escape; all the stars remain apart while the sun and moon are eclipsed. — *Hindi*

Will 10 stars dotted around be equal to the moon by herself? — *Malay*

He who has the moon cares not for the stars. — *Arabic*

Moonlight cannot penetrate into the hollow of a bamboo, no wisdom can enlighten a fool. — *Bengali*

In the old moon, a cloudy morning bodes a fair afternoon. — *Scottish*

Moth

There is never iron so hard that rust will not corrode it; there is no cloth so fine that moths will not eat it. — *Scottish*

A moth holds no clothes in honor. — *Swahili*

The moth that dashes into the flame and burns itself has itself to blame. — *Chinese*

The moth does mischief to the finest garment. — *Italian*

Mountain

Mountains are smooth at a distance, rugged when near.

When we cross one mountain another appears. — *Arabic*

Mountains do not come nearer to mountains, but men do to men. — *Turkish*

Two people may meet but two mountains never. — *German*

A vacant mind is open to all suggestions, as the hollow mountain returns all sounds. — *Chinese*

Silence may defy a mountain. — *Tamil*

The storm may uproot the trees, but not the mountains.

The highest mountain does not reject grains of sand; everything large is made of small amounts. — *Chinese*

No mountain without mist; no man of merit without detractors. — *Turkish*

The mountains in rain and mist amid snow are easy to look at, but difficult to recreate. — *Chinese*

It is better to say mountain than to climb it. — *Welsh*

You cannot have a large valley without first having a large mountain. — *Korean*

Gold lies deep in the mountain, dirt on the highway. — *Germany*

If a dog barks at a mountain, will the mountain be injured or the dog? — *Tamil*

It is better to be ashamed below the mountain than on its top. — *Armenian*

A man will carry a mountain on his head for the sake of gain. — *Hindi*

You cannot climb a mountain by a level road. — *Norwegian*

Without ascending the mountain, you cannot judge the height of heaven; without descending into the valley, you cannot judge the depth of the earth. — *Chinese*

With a mote in the eye, one cannot see the Himalayas. — *Japanese*

A mountain can be hidden by straw. — *Hindi*

It is easy to throw a mountain into the sea after separating one stone from another. — *Welsh*

Behind the mountain there are people, too. — *Swedish*

Where the mind inclines, the feet lead. Love climbs mountains. — *Arabic*

Mouse

Either a man or a mouse.

The mouse who only has one hole is easily taken.

A lion may be obligated to a mouse.

A small mouse can creep under a great corn stack.

A mouse in time may bite a cable in half. — *German*

What does the mouse care about the price of grain since it has its nest in the mill? — *Persian*

The mice do not joke with the kitten. — *Spanish*

It is a bold mouse that makes his nest in the cat's ear. — *Danish*

The mouse is the cat's prey. — *Hindi*

The mouse does not leave a cat's house with a full belly. — *Spanish*

No house without a mouse, no barn without corn, no rose without a thorn. — *German*

The mouse is bridled in his house. — *Arabic*

The mouse is mistress of her own mansion. — *Gaelic*

Burn not your house to drive away the mice.

When mice have had their fill, the meal turns bitter. — *Dutch*

Mule

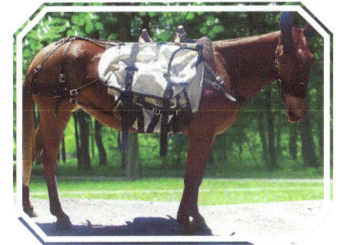

Mules make a great fuss about their ancestors having been horses. — *German*

Tether a mule near a donkey and it will learn either to "hee" or "haw". — *Arabic*

The old mule is not scared at the jingling of bells. — *Arabic*

The horse remains in the stable, the mule in the field.

All mules have big ears.

He asked the old mule: "Who is your father?" He said: "My uncle is a horse." — *Arabic*

Nature

Nature and love cannot be hidden. — *German*

An enemy to beauty is a foe to nature.

Nature requires little, but offers much. — *German*

We do not have to rub down a pearl on a polishing stone. What is beautiful by nature needs no adorning. — *Hindi*

The earth lasts a thousand years, but changes masters continually. — *Chinese*

Everything which comes from heaven, the earth receives it. — *Turkish*

Everything will determine itself according to nature. — *Scottish*

The green hills always remain as witness of the past and present, but fresh water cannot wash away the right and wrong. — *Chinese*

Rivers do not drink up their water, nor trees eat up their fruit, rain does not fall in some places only, the wealth of the virtuous is for others. — *Burmese*

Water has its source, the tree has a root. — *Chinese*

Oaks may fall, while reeds may brave a storm. — *Persian*

The tree gives shade to him who chops it down, the earth supports him who digs it. — *Tamil*

The hills and rivers are easily changed, but a person's disposition is difficult to be moved.

A wise man likes the water, the pious man the hills. — *Chinese*

Every reed will not make a pipe.

Flowers and fruit grow plentifully, the tree depending on a good soil; but depending on a good man, great merit springs into existence. —*Burmese*

Who stands still in mud sticks in it. —*Chinese*

Two watermelons are not held in one hand.

Though the sky of this tear-stained world is overcast with clouds, the light of truth shines in the heart. —*Japanese*

Every pumpkin is known by its stem.

All the stars in the sky face the north, all the rivers of the world flow eastward. —*Chinese*

A bunch of grapes has but one stalk.

We don't gather figs from thistles.

A whole bushel of wheat is made up of single grains.

What flowers are to gardens, spices to food and gems to a garment is what stars are to heaven.

In the sandal trees are serpents. In the waters are lotuses, but alligators also. In our enjoyments are envious spices. No pleasures are unimpeded. —*Hindi*

None but the bird interprets well the volume of the rose; not every reader of a leaf knows its importance. —*Persian*

As birds are made to fly and rivers to run so the soul to follow duty. —*Hindi*

Fire and water are good servants, but bad masters.

Cold sends us to the fire; heat sends us to the shade. —*Chinese*

A fog cannot be dispelled by a fan. —*Japanese*

Does fog have a skeleton? —*Korean*

The opening flower blooms alike in all places: the moon sheds an equal radiance on every mountain and every river. Evil exists only in the heart of man; all other things show the benevolence of heaven towards the human race. — *Chinese*

Rivers and hills of the universe do not change, but their ancient and modern names are all different. — *Chinese*

The bright moon in the water, a flower in a mirror, for a while they seem to be real, but suddenly they prove to be false. — *Chinese*

Night

Night is blind. — *Arabic*

Night is the day of the wicked. — *Turkish*

The evening crowns the day. — *Italian*

If you sing before breakfast, you'll cry at night.

Evening song with drinks: morning song with coughs. — *Swedish*

A drunken night makes a cloudy morning. — *Scottish*

Lust is night; knowledge, light. — *Bengali*

Night is the mother of plots. — *Welsh*

Seldom is there any good from wandering at night. — *Welsh*

Where there is fear of the tiger it is evening. — *Bengali*

Beware of winds and waves by day, of thieves by night. — *Chinese*

The darkest time is just before day.

When night comes fear is at the door; when day comes fear is on the hills. — *Pashto*

The dog guards the night, the rooster rules the morning. — *Chinese*

A rainbow in the morning is the shepherd's warning, rainbow at night is the shepherd's delight. — *Scottish*

Though the night be dark, the hand does not miss the mouth. — *Pashto*

The night is long for the sleepless, the journey is endless for the weary. — *Bengali*

The words of the night are coated with butter; as soon as the day shines upon them, they melt away. — *Arabic*

Night sends crows home. — *Welsh*

Men who never violate their consciences are not afraid if you knock at their door at midnight. — *Chinese*

Nightingale

Even in a golden cage, the nightingale deplores its native land. — *Armenian*

Nightingales can sing their own song the best.

The nightingale lays its young in the crow's nest, but the young do not behave as crows. — *Bengali*

A nightingale won't sing in a cage.

The nightingale and the cuckoo sing both in one month.

The desire of the garden never leaves the heart of the nightingale. — *Persian*

There is nothing so loving as the nightingale. — *Welsh*

Only the nightingale can understand the rose. — *Marathi*

Everybody thinks his own cuckoo sings better than another's nightingale. — *Italian*

Ocean

The whole ocean is made up of single drops.

Leave a wave that dashes against itself. — *Malay*

The tide will take away what the ebb brings.

Every tide has its ebb. —*German*

Time and tide wait for no man.

It is hard to track the path the ship follows in the ocean. —*Danish*

It is hard to fight with the wide ocean. —*German*

As the stars in heaven are numberless, so are the waves of the ocean. —*Bengali*

From the middle of the ocean, no one can see the shore; coming danger also is not perceived in the midst of prosperity. —*Bengali*

When the storm abates, the waves roar. —*Icelandic*

Owl

The owl is the king of the night.

If you follow the owl you will be led to a ruined place. —*Arabic*

The owl does not praise the light, nor the wolf the dog. —*Danish*

Darkness wakens the owl. —*Scottish*

The owl is not accounted the wiser for living reservedly.

The gravest bird is an owl. —*Scottish*

Ox

There's another twist in the ox's horn. —*Gaelic*

The hired ox cannot complain. —*Welsh*

When the ox is leanest, he is best for work. —*Welsh*

The ox feels the pain, the crow feels hunger. — *Tamil*

The ox is held by the horn, and a man by his word. — *Spanish*

A man must plow with such oxen as he has.

He who has neither ox nor cow, plows all night and has nothing in the morning. — *Spanish*

What can a stout ox do with a bad plow? — *Turkish*

A man is ignorant of his own failings as the ox is unconscious of his great strength. — *Chinese*

The ox when weariest treads surest.

An old ox will find a shelter for himself.

Old oxen tread hard. — *German*

Rotten straw does not injure a strong ox. — *Armenian*

The ox that ploughs is not to be muzzled. — *Arabic*

The ox knows his owner, and the ass his owner's stall. — *Chinese*

It's in the rainy season that an ox needs its tail.

An ox when he is free, licks himself at his leisure. — *Spanish*

Nothing so gentle as an ox, nothing so unruly as a steer. — *Welsh*

Before trying to ride horseback, one should learn to ride on oxen. — *Japanese*

He who leads an ox to water must first wet his own feet. — *Chinese*

Peacock

What is the use of a peacock strutting in the forest? — *Malay*

What the peacock has too little on his head, he has too much on this tail. — *German*

When the peacock loudly bawls, soon we will get both rain and squalls.

The sluggard, like the peacock, is afraid of rain.

When March comes in with an adder's head, it goes out with a peacock's tail.

The peacock is delighted with his body, but ashamed of his feet. —*Hindi*

The bird has put on peacock's plumes; the poor man apes the rich. —*Bengali*

When all men praised the peacock for his beautiful tail, the birds cried out with one consent: "Look at his legs! And, what a voice!" —*Japanese*

As proud as a peacock.

Pig

A pig is the richest animal; everything is a piece of gold to him.

Feed a pig and you'll have a hog.

A hog that is stuck in the mud never relaxes until he has made others like himself.

The lazy pig does not eat ripe pears. —*Italian*

The hog knows well what sort of tree to rub himself against.

A hog is always thinking of washing.

The thief and the hog have one road. —*Bengali*

As willful as a pig that will neither lead nor drive.

Rich men spend their time on books, after pigs, a poor man looks. —*Chinese*

To raise a son who will not study is not as good as raising a pig. —*Chinese*

Build a sty before you buy a pig. —*Russian*

A pig cannot stay out of the dirt; a thief cannot keep his fingers still. —*Bengali*

When the pig has had a belly full, it upsets the trough. —*Dutch*

Plants

In the garden more grows than the garden shows. — *Spanish*

Even the worst tea is sweet when first made from the new leaf. — *Japanese*

Plants of learning must be watered with the rain of tears. — *Tamil*

Timely blossoms, timely fruit. — *German*

The bean forgets its pod. — *Malay*

Two cornstalks never are equal in height. — *Swahili*

Nothing will grow if the seed be not sown. — *Japanese*

A low hedge is easily leapt over.

Are only large peppers hot? — *Korean*

Where the hedge is lowest, everyone goes over. — *German*

A good bush never comes from a bad plant. — *Spanish*

Shrubs and plants flourish year after year though unknown to fame, so do not believe that a man of character will remain poor all his life. — *Chinese*

The sweetest grapes hang the highest. — *German*

If the plant is not pulled up by the roots, it will revive. — *Chinese*

Fools are not planted or sowed; they grow of themselves. — *Russian*

Deeds are fruits, while words are only leaves.

If the flower is good, the fruit will be good. — *German*

Big chillies have no pungency, big talkers have no knowledge. —*Bengali*

Woods have ears and fields have eyes. —*German*

A bramble does not produce grapes. —*Russian*

Those who creep through brushes must expect to meet with briars.

As a green and flourishing plant may be bent by the gardener, so may the wise be inclined by good arguments to be good; but no reasoning can change the purpose of a fool; as a tough and stubborn tree may be broken, but it cannot be bent. —*Sinhalese*

Watering the branches and leaves is not like nursing the roots. —*Chinese*

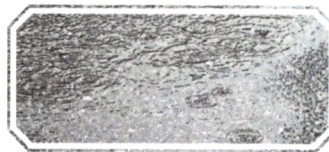

Rabbit

Who chases two rabbits catches neither. —*Japanese*

To excite a fierce dog to capture a lame rabbit is to attack a contemptible enemy. —*Chinese*

He is like a rabbit—fat and lean in 24 hours.

When the rabbit has escaped, comes the advice. —*Spanish*

Rain

Rain breaks no bones. —*Welsh*

A wise man carries his cloak in fair weather, a fool wants his in the rain. —*Scottish*

Rain before 7, clear after 11.

Mist in autumn is a sign of rain.

It rains not as it thunders. — *Pashto*

By constant rain, the dikes burst, by constant nagging, strife comes forth. — *Bengali*

Small rain eventually fills a pond.

Small rain lays a great dust.

Heavy rain scatters mist. — *Gaelic*

Rain from heaven is better than any watering. — *Spanish*

The brown rain at the fall of the leaf; the black rain at the spring of the roots; and the gray rain of May: the three worst of the waters. — *Gaelic*

The mountain has a cap on; that is the rain coming. — *Scottish*

A little rain calms a great wind. — *German*

Falling rain cannot be bent, knowledge gained is permanent. — *Bengali*

When it rains in August, it rains honey and wine. — *Spanish*

Ground that is rained on hardens. — *Japanese*

Misfortune doesn't threaten like rain.

After rain comes sunshine. — *German*

Rainbow

A rainbow in the evening means fine weather. — *Welsh*

A rainbow in the east will be followed by a fine day; in the west by a raining day. — *Chinese*

If there will be a rainbow in the eve, it will rain and leave; but a rainbow in the morrow will neither lend nor borrow.

Rainbows with the new moon, rain until the end. — *Welsh*

A rainbow at noon will bring rain very soon. — *Scottish*

Rat

The rat knows the rat's road. — *Chinese*

The rat rattles the lid and makes his nature known.

If you talk about tomorrow's matters, the rats above the ceiling will laugh. — *Japanese*

The passage of a single rat is nothing, but it soon becomes a thoroughfare. — *Arabic*

Ivory does not come from a rat's mouth. — *Chinese*

The blind rat gets hollow grain.

An old rat won't go into the trap. — *German*

When the cat is safe in the forest, the rat says, "She's my wife." — *Hindi*

Boat rats seek their food in the boat's compartments. — *Chinese*

Raven

Grain sown does not grow if the raven has seen it. — *Armenian*

The raven chides blackness.

He who takes the raven for a guide shall light upon carrion. — *Persian*

Judgment spares the raven, but hunts down the dove.

Whenever the raven flies over one's head, there must be before us some trouble to dread. — *Persian*

No doves come out of raven eggs. — *Icelandic*

River

Rivers need a spring.

A great river makes no noise. — *Turkish*

Deep rivers move with silence, shallow brooks are noisy. — *German*

When the river is silent it is either empty, very full or flooded. — *Spanish*

Water always runs to the river.

The river does not swell with clear water. — *Italian*

Whoever walks on the river's bank will himself fall in. — *Pashto*

A smooth river washes away its banks.

After high floods come low ebbs. — *German*

Sooner will two men meet than two riverbanks. — *Welsh*

Mountains do not hinder a journey so much as rivers. — *Chinese*

Is it kind to abandon someone in the middle of a river? — *Tamil*

Whoever knows the right methods is equally able to do both a great and small feat, just as the current of a river can uproot trees as well as grasses.

Follow the river and you'll get to the sea.

As the rivers pour their waters back again into the sea, so what a man has lent is returned to him again. — *Chinese*

The course of a river is not to be changed.

All rivers do what they can for the sea.

The greatest rivers must run into the sea. — *German*

All the rivers flow into the sea and yet it is not full. — *Chinese*

Though you may sing a filthy song on its bank, the Ganges is not defiled. — *Bengali*

Great floods come from great mountains and go to great rivers.—*Pashto*

Where hills are lofty, rivers are deep.—*Chinese*

If a river is dried up, do not prepare your feet?—*Armenian*

Though the river is large, boats still come into collision.—*Chinese*

When drops collect, a large river is made out them.—*Pashto*

A loving disposition is a river without a ripple.—*Tamil*

Many shun the brook and fall into the river.—*German*

The river produces a variety of fish and flowers, but though they proceed from the same water, they have a different taste and smell.

Throw him into a river and he will rise with a fish in his mouth.—*Arabic*

Rook

Bring down the nests and the rooks will flee away.—*Scottish*

The sound of a bell does not drive away rooks.—*Italian*

The raven is fair when the rook is not by it.—*Danish*

When the rooks are silent, the swans begin to sing.—*Danish*

Rose

The rose does not spring from the tears of mourning.

A pearl becomes red by the nearness of a rose, but never a rose will become white by contact with a pearl. Tis not the lower, but the more noble that readily recognizes and takes home for profit the high qualities of others.—*Hindu*

For the rose, the thorn is watered.—*Arabic*

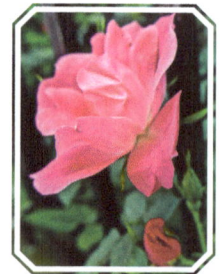

The rose from rose is born, the thorn from thorn.—*Pashto*

Truths and roses have thorns about them.

Gather the rose and leave the thorn.—*Italian*

For the rose, the thorn is often plucked.—*Italian*

Whoever will gather roses must not be afraid of the thorns.

You must be under obligations to a hundred thorns for the sake of one rose.—*Persian*

A rose comes forth from thorns.—*Arabic*

If you lie upon roses when young, you will be upon thorns when old.

Knowledge is not gained on a bed of roses.—*Turkish*

If you desire ease in this life, keep your secrets undisclosed like the modest rosebud. Take warning from that lovely flower that, by expanding its hitherto hidden beauties when in full bloom, gives its leaves and its happiness to the winds.—*Persian*

The fairest rose will wither at last.

Sand

There is no twisting a rope of sand.

Many grains of sand will sink a ship.—*Danish*

He counts the sands of the desert as beads on his fingers.—*Arabic*

Striking the purse of another is like a blow on a sand hill.—*Arabic*

A wall of sand and the love of the vicious have the same fate.—*Bengali*

Whoever builds on the mob, builds on sand.—*Italian*

Friendship with a mean person is a wall of sand.—*Arabic*

He extracts oil from the sands of the desert.—*Persian*

Sand sharpens a knife, a stone the axes, good words a good man, a thrashing a rogue.—*Bengali*

Whoever offends, writes on sand; who is offended, on marble.— *Italian*

What you give, is written in sand; what you take, is taken with an iron hand.—*German*

Sand will not hold water; a blind man cannot see the road.—*Bengali*

Sand forms the mountains, moments make the year.

Sea

All water runs to the sea.—*German*

The sea refuses no river.

Unlucky at sea, unlucky at land.—*Welsh*

Even the sea, great as it is, grows calm.—*German*

A good pilot is not known when the sea is calm and the weather is fair.—*Danish*

Praise the sea and keep on land.—*Italian*

Go to the sea if you would fish well.—*Italian*

If a cup of fresh water is poured into the sea, will the saltwater become fresh?—*Malay*

Drop by drop the sea may be exhausted.—*Spanish*

The seas are not still while the winds blow, neither can people be spiritually alive while their affections are upon the earth.

The sea has not a shore, neither is there a bridge over it, nor any other means of crossing it.

A man is not always known by his looks, nor is the sea measured with a bushel.—*Chinese*

If you want that which is in the sea, go and wait for it on the beach.—*Swahili*

Many kinds of persons sail across the sea.—*Icelandic*

Be content, the sea has enough fish.

He that is at sea must either sail or sink.—*Danish*

To do good to the ungrateful is to throw rosewater into the sea.

More men are drowned in the bowl than in the sea.—*German*

To beg of a miser is to dig a trench in the sea.—*Turkish*

A mother's love will draw up from the depths of the sea.—*Russian*

No one can complain of the sea who is twice shipwrecked.—*German*

He is like the anchor that is always in the sea, yet does not learn to swim.—*Italian*

He that will not sail until he has a full, fair wind, will lose many a voyage.

A smooth sea never made a skillful mariner.

Seasons

Everything is good in its season.—*Italian*

There are not two summers in one year.—*Russian*

Summer moments always pass quickly.—*Norwegian*

The year disappears like lightning.—*Turkish*

Spring is sooner recognized by plants than men.—*Chinese*

Change of the weather is the talk of fools.—*Spanish*

Fine weather makes every season summer.—*Welsh*

That which blossoms in the spring will bring forth fruit in the autumn.

The poor man's youth, the summer's sun, the winter's moon; these three pass unenjoyed.—*Hindi*

Every season has its reason.—*Scottish*

Scorpion

Whoever pats scorpions with the hand of compassion receives punishment. —*Persian*

The poison of a scorpion is in its tail, of a fly in its head, but of a bad man in his whole body.

A scorpion's luggage is on its back.

On seeing a lizard, a scorpion puts down its stinger.

Bad relatives are scorpions. —*Persian*

One gets eternal sleep if bitten by a serpent, but weeps if bitten by a scorpion. —*Hindi*

The scorpion stings him who helps it out of the fire. —*Tamil*

We were prepared for the serpent but gave no thought to the scorpion. —*Arabic*

He who is stung by a scorpion is frightened at its shadow. —*Spanish*

Sheep

A sheep was never known to climb a tree. —*Chinese*

The sheep does not remember its father; it only thinks about grass. —*Russian*

When one sheep leads the way, all the rest follow. —*Chinese*

Sheep are not designed for the shepherd, but the shepherd is for service of the sheep. —*Persian*

Straying shepherd, straying sheep. —*German*

He cast a sheep's eye at her.

A sheep also can lift its tail.

It's a foolish sheep that makes the wolf its confessor. —*Italian*

One lamb makes a small flock. —*Norwegian*

One scabbed sheep infects the flock.

A lamb is as dear to a poor man as an ox to the rich.

The sheep that wanders from the flock, the wolf seizes. —*Turkish*

Whoever makes himself a sheep, the wolf devours him. —*French*

All the sheep are not for the wolf. —*German*

The lone sheep is in danger of the wolf.

Although the sheep may wear the tiger's skin, if it sees a wolf, it trembles. —*Chinese*

It is better to give the wool than the sheep. —*Italian*

The strength of a ram is in his head. —*Welsh*

A sheep's bite is never more than skin deep. —*German*

Even a sheep will bite a man without a stick.

Nothing disturbs the sheepfold like a strange sheep. —*Arabic*

Sky

A small-minded person looks at the sky through a reed. —*Japanese*

A red sky in all directions indicates bad weather. —*Spanish*

Life is arched with changing skies, rarely are they what they seem.

Neither winter not summer rests always in the sky. —*Italian*

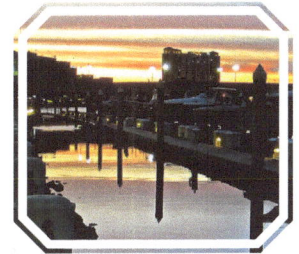

The eyebrow of the new moon will not become green with the dye of the sky. —*Persian*

Whoever throws a stone at the sky, may have it fall on his head. —*Italian*

The sky is not less blue because the blind man doesn't see it. —*Danish*

A gloom comes with a storm.—*Welsh*

If you don't believe in the gods, only observe the thunder's roar.—*Chinese*

Much morning dew makes for blue skies.—*German*

Snail

The snail deserves the end of its journey.—*Welsh*

A snail is precious due to the pearl of its shell, fools have nothing that can bring them to greatness.—*Tamil*

Snails moving on bushes or grass are signs of rain.

When black snails cross your path, black clouds will have much moisture.

The first snail going with you, and the first lamb meeting you, bodes a good year.—*Scottish*

A man travels as far in a day as a snail in a hundred years.—*French*

Its shell follows the snail wherever it goes.

Snake

Snakes have no chiefs.—*Tamil*

Although a serpent has little eyes, he sees very well.

If a tame snake goes into a jungle, it will become a wild one.—*Tamil*

Of a serpent whole and healthy, the strength lies ever in his tail.—*Welsh*

Although you feed a snake with milk, it will yield poison.—*Tamil*

Warm a frozen serpent and it will bite you first.—*Armenian*

Provocation is a stone thrown at a cobra.

Look before you leap, for snakes among sweet flowers do creep.

If a snake creeps around a root, it does not thereby lose its venom.—*Malay*

If a snake wants to live, it doesn't journey upon the high road.

Are there any snakes who will not bite those who step on them? — *Tamil*

A snake bites, but gets nothing in its mouth.

A pleasant voice brings a snake out of its hole. — *Persian*

Draw the snake from its hole using another man's hand. — *Spanish*

A snake cannot enter his hole until he straightens himself. — *Persian*

Like a snake in a bamboo tube, a crooked nature is hard to change. — *Chinese*

A bamboo stick is king to a snake. — *Tamil*

The serpent brings forth nothing but a little serpent. — *Arabic*

A young snake is more poisonous and vigorous than an old one. — *Tamil*

No man can remain with a snake in a cage.

A greedy man is like a serpent wishing to swallow an elephant. — *Chinese*

The blind man does not fear the snake. — *Japanese*

Whoever has seen a black serpent is afraid of a black stick. — *Armenian*

A snake bites for fear of its life. — *Pashto*

One who is bitten by a snake does not twice walk in the grass. — *Chinese*

When bitten by a snake, does medicine used for scorpion bites help? — *Tamil*

When it is time for the snake to die, it goes onto the road. — *Pashto*

Be a serpent except in the poison. — *Japanese*

He who keeps malice harbors a viper in his heart.

A viper is never grateful. — *Bengali*

He was a quiet as a snake in a box.

There is poison in a serpent, but there is more venom in a wicked man; for there are remedies for the one, but there is no cure for the other.—*Sinhalese*

Friendship with the wicked is like playing with snakes.

It is said the snake, afraid of the charmer, sought the friendship of the rat.—*Tamil*

The snake only knows where its feet are.

If you whistle at night, snakes will come forth.—*Japanese*

Digging for a worm, up rose a snake.—*Bengali*

Of what use is a tree, bending under the weight of its fruit, if a serpent lies nestling at its root while sending forth poison from his fang?—*Hindu*

Snow

A snow year, a rich year.

The feet are slow when the head wears snow.—*Scottish*

Sweep the snow from your own door, spy not at the frost on another's tiles.—*Chinese*

Unjustly got wealth is snow sprinkled with hot water; lands improperly obtained are but sandbanks in a stream.—*Chinese*

Corn is as comfortable under snow as an old man is under his fur coat.—*Russian*

He wishes to hide his footprints, and yet walks upon the show.—*Chinese*

If the icy snow carries you at midsummer, then you can expect a late spring.—*Icelandic*

Thaw reveals what has been hidden by snow.—*Dutch*

Lies melt like snow.—*German*

From snow, whether cooked or pounded, you will get nothing by water.—*Italian*

Sparrow

A sparrow in hand is worth a pheasant that flies by.—*Russian*

Whoever is afraid of the sparrows should never sow seeds.

The sparrow builds in the martin's nest.

Old sparrows are hard to tame.—*German*

Sparrows should not dance with cranes since their legs are too short.—*Danish*

Two sparrows upon one ear of wheat cannot agree.

Spider

It is more easily broken than the web of a spider.—*Arabic*

Big flies break the spider's web.—*Italian*

Friends tie their purses with a spider's web.

A spider dances by means of a stick.

Long, single separate spider webs on grass are a sign of frost next night.—*Gaelic*

If good fortune you would win, let the spider live and spin.

The spider's web lets the rat escape and catches the fly.—*Spanish*

Squirrel

A squirrel ascends by climbing. — *Tamil*

Nothing is lively, but a squirrel. — *Welsh*

The hunted squirrel runs to the tree.

Not to distinguish properly between the beautiful and ugly, is like attaching a dog's tail to a squirrel's body. — *Chinese*

The abilities of the flying squirrel are easily exhausted. — *Chinese*

Quick and nimble, more like a bear than a squirrel.

Stars

The stars in heaven are nearer to you. — *Arabic*

Stars are not seen by sunshine. — *German*

A star, however willing, cannot help the moon. — *Chinese*

Cold night, stars bright.

The heavens are studded with stars. — *French*

As the stars, so man appears little at a distance. — *Japanese*

One may point at a star, but not pull at it.

As the light of a single star tinges the mountains of many regions, so a single unguarded expression affects the virtue of a person's whole life. — *Chinese*

When the stars begin to huddle, the earth will soon become a puddle.

A mariner must have his eye upon rock and sands as well as upon the North Star.

Even a small star shines in the darkness.— *Finnish*

Can 10 scattered stars equal the single moon?— *Malay*

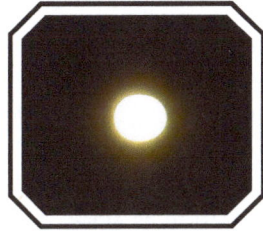

The sky full of stars depends on one moon.— *Chinese*

Flowers are the poetry of earth, as stars are the poetry of heaven.

Stones

A rock not moved by an iron lever will be opened by the root of a green tree.— *Tamil*

The bold man is harder than a stone.— *Welsh*

The egg fights with the rock.— *Chinese*

Frequent blows will break the stone.— *Welsh*

The constant rope cut the stone.— *Swahili*

Even stones may be dissolved, the heart of a fool not.— *Tamil*

Those who throw stones will have stones thrown at them.— *Korean*

Water on a stone will wet it, but enters not.

Quiet water splits a stone.— *Bengali*

Truth as a stone dissolves not in water.— *Bengali*

A stone turning is sure to be chipped.— *Arabic*

Moss does not attach itself to stones that are continually rolling in a river.— *Malay*

The rougher the stones, the firmer the wall.— *Welsh*

Those who will not be ruled by the rudder must be ruled by the rock. —*Cornish*

A word and a stone thrown once launched cannot be recalled. —*Spanish*

A stone is rolled up a hill by great exertions but is easily thrown down.

Do not throw a stone into the well out of which you have drunk.

Don't speak of stones to a fool or he will throw them at your head. —*Turkish*

Virtue is always exposed to envy; we don't cast stones at a barren tree.

A reward given to one worthy is engraved in stone, but when given to the unkind, it is written in water. —*Tamil*

Biting a stone breaks the teeth.

For neighbors to keep up a friendly tone, is equal to finding a precious stone. —*Chinese*

It is better to carry stones on one's head from the tops of high mountains than to be under an obligation to anyone. —*Pashto*

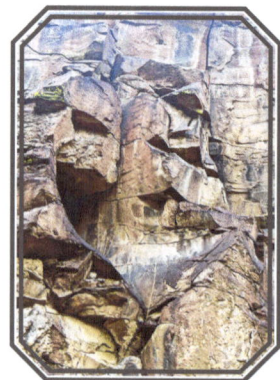

Among men some are jewels and some are pebbles.

The past is underneath the stone. —*Pashto*

We should build with the stones we have. —*Swedish*

The gem cannot be polished without friction, nor a man perfected without trials. —*Chinese*

A little stone overturns a great cart. —*Italian*

Streams

Sweet water cannot come from a foul stream. —*Persian*

The heart of the worthless is an unmovable and changeless as a mountain stream. —*Chinese*

It is easy going with the stream.

The stream that has passed down does not come back to its former channel. —*Persian*

Mistrust the water that does not warble and the stream that does not chirp. —*Armenian*

It is hard to swim against the stream. —*German*

Sun

Every light is not the sun. —*German*

The lamp gives no light in the presence of the sun. —*Persian*

Nothing beneath the sun is lasting. —*Swedish*

You cannot stop the sun by standing before it.

When the sun shines no one minds it, but when the sun is eclipsed everyone thinks about it.

Knowledge overcomes ignorance as sunlight to darkness.

As the sun, the eye of the whole world is not sullied by the defects of external objects, so the inner soul of all beings is not sullied by the misery of the world.

The light of learning is the day of mind.

As the sun's shadow shifts, so there is no permanence on earth.

When the sun shines, the shadow dies.

Sun, moon and stars rise; man gets up. —*German*

In heaven, there are not two suns; among the people, there are not two kings; in a family there are not two masters, among the honorable there are not two supremes. —*Chinese*

The sun can be seen by nothing, but its own light.

The sun sets, but misfortune never sets.

The flower's enemy is the sun, and the butter's is the bug. —*Hindi*

Better one sun than a myriad of stars. — *Welsh*

The sun is not hidden from view by the fingers. —*Pashto*

I best know the sun of my own country. —*Arabic*

The sun is still beautiful though ready to set.

The morning sun never lasts a day.

Swallow

The small birds look around them and eat; the swallow goes to sleep without apprehension. He who possesses an enlarged and sedate mind will have great happiness, but the man whose schemes are deep will have a great depth of misery. —*Chinese*

In the year when the swallows do not return to their old nest, there will be a fire in that house. —*Japanese*

When a swallow has its nest on a tent, it cannot rest in comfort. —*Chinese*

One swallow doesn't make a summer. —*Spanish*

When property changes owners, it is just like a swallow entering another person's house. —*Chinese*

The swallow plastering up its nest is labor lost.

Swan

There is none so proud as the swan. —*Welsh*

It is not for the swan to teach eaglets to sing. —*Danish*

The uneducated in society are as crows among swans. —*Hindi*

Can the swallows know the wild swan's intention? —*Chinese*

A rare bird upon the earth is like a black swan.

The swan feeds on pearls or fasts. —*Hindi*

Thorns

The thorn comes forth with its point forward.

A pliant thorn will not penetrate. —*Tamil*

A thorn is small, but he who has felt it does not forget it. —*Italian*

Does one sharpen the thorns? —*Malay*

Those who sow thorns can only reap prickles. —*Turkish*

A sluggard is like a hedge of thorns. —*Tamil*

He that sows thistles shall reap prickles. —*Russian*

He knows well where the thorn pricked him. —*Italian*

Thistles and thorns prick sore, but evil tongues prick more. —*Dutch*

He that plants thorns shall not gather roses. —*Persian*

The roses fall and the thorns remain. —*Italian*

Who sows thorns should not go barefoot. —*French*

Tiger

The tiger is the king of beasts. —*Chinese*

Do not excite a tiger.

Press hard on a tiger and he injures you. —*Chinese*

Tigers do not live in flocks.

When a tiger is hungry will he eat grass? —*Tamil*

Who washes a tiger's face?

An old tiger keeps close to the village, an old man hugs the fire. —*Bengali*

What matters to the tiger if he is in his native jungle or another? —*Tamil*

If a man's destiny is crooked, even in a jungle of dark grass, a tiger attacks him. —*Bengali*

He sits like a tiger withdrawing his claws. —*Malay*

Better not to fire on the tiger than to wound it. —*Russian*

If you a raise a tiger in your home, it will tear you up when it gets larger. —*Chinese*

The doctor who cured the striped tiger of his sickness became his prey. —*Tamil*

Although one may escape the claws of the tiger, even the pricking of its whisker will prove malignant. —*Tamil*

It's a shameful thing if a tiger cub becomes a kitten. —*Malay*

If you do not enter a tiger's den, you cannot get his cubs. —*Chinese*

A tiger comes from a cub. —*Hindi*

The tiger will not eat its own cubs. —*Malay*

Tigers and deer do not stroll together. —*Chinese*

A jungle inhabited by fierce tigers is better than a country ruled by a cruel tyrant. —*Tamil*

Tigers in the eastern hills will catch men just as well as tigers in the western hills. —*Chinese*

Though a tiger may not devour men, his dreadful appearance frightens them. —*Chinese*

Man has no intention of harming the tiger, but the tiger is bent on injuring man. —*Chinese*

If you know there are tigers in the hills, don't go there. —*Chinese*

It is easy to ascend a hill and catch a tiger, but it is difficult to ask a favor. —*Chinese*

In painting a tiger, you paint his skin, but not his bones; knowing a man, you know his face, but not his heart. —*Chinese*

The crouching of the tiger is the prelude to spring. —*Tamil*

An evil man relying on authority is like a tiger taking refuge in a corner of a hill. —*Chinese*

The goat is the prey of the tiger. —*Hindi*

The tiger on the plain is insulted by the dogs. —*Chinese*

The tiger and the goat are watered at one place.

A wicked man is like a tiger with wings; he will devour anyone he likes. —*Chinese*

The jungle will not be without a tiger.

Through a gap in the fence, the tiger enters; separation among relatives lets in strangers. —*Bengali*

Tortoise

The tortoise would fly if it had wings.

Urged to pay, he resembles a tortoise. —*Chinese*

It is wanton waste to feed a tortoise with barley.

The slow gait of the tortoise takes him far.

The fly that bites the tortoise breaks its beak. —*Italian*

The turtle lays thousands of eggs and no one knows anything about it, but when a hen lays an egg, the whole country rings with noise. —*Malay*

Trees

Whoever plants trees, loves others besides himself.

The tree is a great man, and the young birds are his dependents. —*Swahili*

There are trees on the mountains a thousand years old, but a centenarian among men is hard to find. —*Chinese*

All men have a face, all trees their bark.

People delight to see a noble tree, but if a man becomes great, the sight of him is bitter to them. —*Bengali*

The highest branch is not the safest roost.

There are always people to grab the branches when there are people to carry the spruce. —*Finnish*

From small seeds big trees grow. —*Norwegian*

Trees will not grow until you scatter seed. —*Persian*

The seed of the banyan tree is small, but the tree gives a large shade. —*Tamil*

There is often a withered branch on a green tree. —*Norwegian*

When the tree falls, it leans on its neighbor. —*Swahili*

A miser is a tree with fruit you can't get.

Great trees give more shade than fruit. —*German*

Great trees, as fig trees, make shade for others and stand themselves in the glowing heat of the sun. They bear fruits for others, not for themselves.

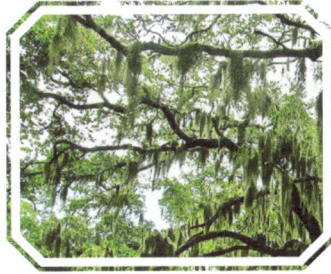

The more a good tree grows, the more shade it gives. — *Greek*

He found shelter in the shade of the tree, and in return, broke its branches. — *Bengali*

Temperance is a tree which has contentment for its root, and peace for its fruit. — *Arabic*

The same tree may produce sour and sweet fruit; the same mother may have stupid and intelligent children. — *Chinese*

Stones and sticks are flung only at fruit-bearing trees. — *Persian*

Such as the tree is, such is the fruit.

Let us be like trees that yield their fruit to those who throw stones at them. — *Persian*

A bad tree does not yield good apples. — *German*

Better be late ripe like the mulberry, than soon in blossom like the almond. — *Spanish*

A tree often transplanted is never full of fruit. — *German*

A tree that bears much fruit droops its head. — *Meiteilon*

The tree of the world has its poisons, but bears two fruits of exquisite flavor: the nectar of poetry and the society of noble men. — *Hindi*

A fig tree looking on a fig tree becomes fruitful. — *Arabic*

The tree feels not the weight of its fruit. — *Bengali*

The tree bears not fruit for itself, nor for itself does the stream collect its waters. For the benefit of others alone does the sage assume a bodily shape. — *Hindi*

Wherever the tree of beneficence takes root, it sends forth branches beyond the sky. — *Persian*

If the tree is well rooted, the wind will not shake it; if it stands upright, it matters not if its shadow is crooked.—*Arabic*

A tree that has just taken root may be pulled up by the strength of a man.—*Persian*

In digging up a tree you must begin with the root.—*Chinese*

Patience is a tree whose root is bitter, but its fruit very sweet.—*Persian*

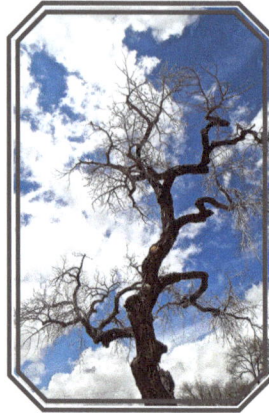

A crooked tree will have a crooked shadow.

Deep roots fear no wind.

When the root is worthless so is the tree.—*German*

When a tree dies at its root, its branches dry up also.—*Swahili*

Remove an old tree and it will wither.—*German*

In an aged man appears ripeness of wisdom, in an old sandal tree is produced the fragrance.—*Hindi*

A young twig is easier twisted than an old tree.

The growth of a mulberry tree corresponds with its early bent.—*Chinese*

The tree must be bent while it is young.—*German*

The tree falls not at the first stroke.

An old tree has a firm core.

When a tree falls, everyone goes to it with their hatchets.—*French*

Many blows fell great trees.— *Norwegian*

An oak is not felled at one chop.

The more a tree is lopped, the higher it grows.—*Pashto*

To fell a tree to catch a blackbird.—*Chinese*

Strike at every tree, yet none is felled. —*Gaelic*

As much as you cut the willow, it will grow stronger.

Before cutting down the forest, is it necessary to consult the axe?

To climb a tree to catch fish is talking much and doing nothing.—*Chinese*

The wood of trees that grow rapidly are not hard.—*Korean*

The sandalwood tree never ceases to exhale its fragrance even when it is felled to the earth. The stately elephant, even in old age never loses his relish for sport. The sugarcane keeps its sweetness, carry it whither you will. A noble man, even under pressure of sharp trial, will never lose his poise and exalted character.

A great tree attracts the wind.—*Chinese*

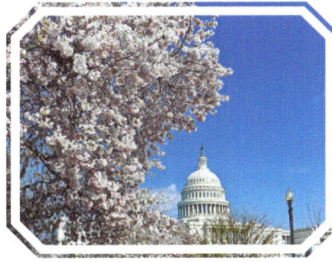

Great trees are good to shelter under.

When a tree is blown down, it shows that the branches are larger than the roots.

There is no place in the sandalwood trees to which a multitude of animals of all places do not rest; serpents at the roots, birds on the tops, apes in the branches, and bees on the flowers.

Although there be an immense number of forests, few are the lands that have growth of sandalwood. So though there are many wise men, the golden sayings are very rare.—*Tibetan*

Patience is a tree whose root is bitter, but its fruit very sweet.—*Persian*

Though the firs of the forest have no granaries, the wide world is before them.—*Chinese*

A short tree stands long.

Great trees keep down the little ones.

The greatest oaks have been little acorns.

Green wood makes a hot fire.

The trees that are close together in a clump and united resist the fiercest winds due to their mutual support.

A single strand of silk does not make a thread, one tree does not make a grove. — *Chinese*

The pine stands afar and whispers to its own forest. — *Russian*

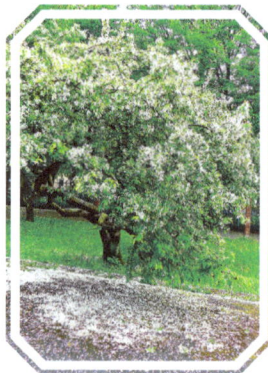

As the fir and the cypress trees can endure snow and frost, so intelligent wisdom can pass over difficulties and dangers. — *Chinese*

Riches are like a tree on a river bank. — *Bengali*

Willows are weak yet they bind other wood. — *Italian*

Trees on the river bank perish every now and then.

Though the white gem is cast into the dirt, its purity cannot be forever soiled; though a good man may live in a vile place, his heart cannot be depraved. As the fir and cypress trees withstand the challenges of the winter, so resplendent wisdom is safe in difficult and dangerous situations. — *Chinese*

Vines

Eggplants do not grow upon melon vines. — *Japanese*

The vine lives by winding itself around the tree. When the tree falls, the vine dies. — *Chinese*

Make the vine poor by pruning off its branches and it will make you rich.

Love, like a creeping vine, withers and dies if it has nothing to embrace. — *Bengali*

Cut your vine with your own hand, but not with the hand of others.

One cow eats another man's vines.

Sow corn in clay and plant vines in sand.—*Spanish*

Every vine must have its stake.

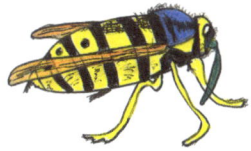

Wasp

Fire drives the wasp out of its nest.—*Italian*

More wasps are caught by honey than vinegar.—*Persian*

One grape and a hundred wasps.—*Persian*

It is not only the worst fruit that is liked by wasps.—*German*

Wasps hunt the honey pot.—*Persian*

Water

Water cut will not split.—*Malay*

A handful of water is not to be grasped.—*Swahili*

What water gives, water takes away.—*Portuguese*

If you want clear water, draw it from the spring.—*German*

He that fixes his mind too much on water, drinks it not.—*Swahili*

Drink the water and know the fountain.—*Chinese*

The water that comes from the same spring cannot be both fresh and salty.

The man who eats the salt must drink the water.—*Korean*

Dirty water does not wash clean.—*German*

Water long stagnant becomes putrid.—*Persian*

If the water is too pure, fish cannot live in it; if a man is too strict, others cannot stand beside him.—*Japanese*

Foul water will quench a fire.

Far off water will not quench a nearby fire.

Any water will put out a fire.—*German*

Water will mingle with water and become one, but the scum goes to the side all the same.—*Malay*

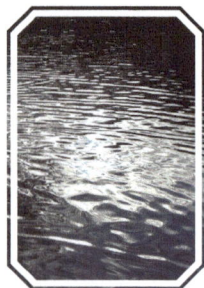

Water washes everything.—*Portuguese*

Don't enter the water where there is no ford.—*Pashto*

A benefit given to the good is like characters engraved on a stone; a benefit given to the evil is like a line drawn on water.

Water from a birch cup in your own land is better than beer from a golden cup in a strange land.—*Finnish*

A little water is enough for clay that is already moistened.—*Persian*

Be not as water which takes the tint of all colors.

We don't feel cold when going into the deep water.—*Malay*

The deepest waters are the most silent.

Boat helps boat, water helps water.—*Chinese*

As the current is slow when the water is deep, so a man of distinction is slow to speak.

Thread cannot pass without a needle, nor the boat cross without water.—*Chinese*

Worldly prosperity is like writing on water.

Water can both sustain and upset a ship.—*Chinese*

Just as high land becomes arid and useless due to the water running off it, so is the man who accomplishes nothing because he is too high and mighty.

A drop of water breaks a stone. — *German*

Men's passions are like water. When water has once overflowed, it cannot easily be restored. When passions have once been indulged, they cannot easily be restrained. Water must be kept in by dikes, so passions must be regulated by the laws of propriety. — *Chinese*

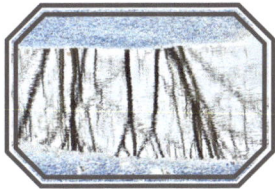

Every path has a puddle.

Water flows towards low places, and man aims high. — *Chinese*

Water does not forget its course. — *Armenian*

Where water has been, water will come again. — *German*

A well is not to be filled with dew. — *Arabic*

Who digs many wells doesn't get sweet water in all of them. — *Swedish*

It is not easy to stop a fire when water is far; friends nearby are better than far off relatives. — *Chinese*

The nature of water varies according to the soil. — *Tamil*

A wise man adapts himself to circumstances, as water shapes itself to the vessel that contains it. — *Chinese*

Water Buffalo

The dust of the water buffalo is lost in that of the elephant. — *Hindi*

A young buffalo need not be taught. — *Malay*

A buffalo makes a house prosper, a cornstalk makes high ground conspicuous. — *Tamil*

If you can't distinguish a cow by night, how can you distinguish a buffalo by night? — *Tamil*

Though the buffalo has large horns, they are on his own head.

For uphill work use a horse, for downhill use a buffalo. — *Hindi*

If the buffalo goes into the dense jungle, the tiger eats him; he who frequents the company of fools risks a beating. —*Bengali*

Water Lily

Every pond will not produce water lilies, nor do sweet-scented trees grow on every hill. It is not every man who is wise. —*Bengali*

The righteous shine among the ignorant as the lilies in a heap of garbage.

Are there water lilies in every pool? —*Bengali*

By the growth of the water lilies, one can tell the depth of the water; by a man's bearing, you can tell his breeding. —*Bengali*

Weeds

The plentiful weeds in this world's path should be uprooted. The obstructive weeds of the mind ought to be removed. —*Chinese*

Bad weeds grow swiftly. —*German*

Bad weeds are not hurt by frost. —*Portuguese*

Bad weeds grow the fastest and last the longest. —*Danish*

No garden is without its weeds.

A good garden may have some weeds.

Weeds need no sowing.

Weeds are likely to grow faster than good herbs.

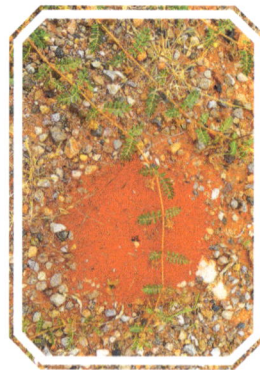

One year's (weed) seed, seven year's weed.

Weeds never die. — *German*

The plant of immortality may lie hidden among weeds, just as a basin of the finest gold may be buried in the mud. — *Chinese*

A man of words and not of deeds, is like a garden full of weeds. — *Scottish*

Wind

The wind cannot be prevented from blowing. — *Russian*

The fair wind blows even if the sailor does not see it. — *Norwegian*

If the wind blows, it enters at every crevice. — *Arabic*

A fair wind at our back is best. — *Norwegian*

No weather is ill if the wind be still.

The waiting man gets the wind behind him. — *Swedish*

The east wind travels where it is supposed to. — *Norwegian*

The east wind is a bitter foe. — *Welsh*

When the wind is in the south, it's in the rain's mouth.

An idle head is a box for the wind.

When the wind is in the south, it blows the bait into the fishes' mouths.

A raging wind only strikes those who are in it. — *Chinese*

High winds blow on high hills. — *Persian*

To grasp the wind is like grasping a shadow. — *Chinese*

Time passes like the wind. — *Portuguese*

A calumnious mouth is a fire in the wind.

Life is a light before the wind. — *Japanese*

Who is free from trouble and care? When the wind blows, even the waves that were calm become crested with foam. — *Chinese*

The wind does not always blow from the same place. — *German*

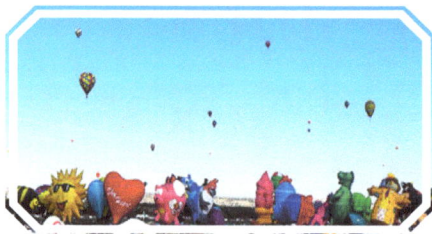

Wealth brought by the wind is scattered by the hurricane. — *Arabic*

If there is no wind, the trees do not rock. — *Malay*

When there is no wind, bushes don't shake. — *Pashto*

You must shift your sail with the wind. — *Italian*

The wind is the friend of a fire burning a forest; it even extinguishes a lamp; in a wicked man, there is no friendship whatsoever. — *Burmese*

It is hard to sail without wind and to grind without water. — *Danish*

Wind and good luck are seldom lasting. — *Spanish*

No wind can do him good who steers for no port. — *French*

A fair-weather friend changes with the wind. — *Spanish*

He who follows when a fair wind blows must follow in a head wind. — *Norwegian*

Come with the wind, go with the water. — *Persian*

Wolf

One wolf does not bite another. — *Spanish*

A hungry wolf is not at rest.

An old wolf is not scared by loud cries. —*German*

The wolf with education becomes no lamb. —*Armenian*

If you want to be friends with a wolf, have a dog nearby. —*Turkish*

He ran from the wolf and fell in with the bear. —*Russian*

Whoever marries a wolf often looks towards the forest. —*Spanish*

Fear has many eyes; he who fears the wolf will not enter the forest. —*Russian*

Cover yourself not with the skin of a wolf, if you don't want to be considered a wolf. —*Spanish*

Make yourself a sheep and the wolf is ready. —*Russian*

As a wolf is like a dog, so a flatterer like a friend.

He who goes with wolves learns to howl. —*Italian*

A sheep in appearance, but a wolf at heart. —*Hindi*

The wolf is always said to be more terrible than he is. —*Italian*

The wolf and the fox are both of one gang. —*Spanish*

The wolf calls the fox a robber. —*German*

While keeping a tiger from the front door, a wolf enters by the back. —*Chinese*

Hunger drives the wolf out of the woods.

If the wolf had stayed in the woods there would have been no commotion and cry after him. —*German*

An old goat should not joke with a wolf. —*Hindi*

News of a wolf makes the wolf bigger than he is. —*German*

The wolf loses his teeth, but not his inclinations. —*Spanish*

When you see a wolf, do not look for his tracks. —*Italian*

A thief knows a thief as a wolf knows a wolf.

He who feeds a wolf strengthens his enemy. — *Danish*

Where the wolf picks up one sheep, he looks for another. — *Portuguese*

The dust raised by the sheep does not choke the wolf.

When the wolf gets among the flock, woe to him who has only one sheep. — *Spanish*

The friend of the wolf is the lazy shepherd. — *Welsh*

Worm

Tread on a worm and it will turn. — *French*

They live like a silkworm in a cocoon, seemingly secure, but in reality helpless.

He sees a glowworm and thinks it's a fire. — *Turkish*

Worms may eat away the heart without its being known but the prick of a finger calls for immediate attention. — *Korean*

Even a worm an inch long has a soul half an inch long. — *Japanese*

Even an earth worm will resent being stepped on. — *Korean*

Wren

The wren spreads its feet wide in its own house. — *Gaelic*

None so brisk as the wren. — *Welsh*

He who disturbs the wren's nest, with health he will never be blessed. — *Welsh*

Various Animals

They are only horses and cows in clothes who neglect the study of the past and present. —*Chinese*

The most dangerous of wild beasts is a slanderer, of tame ones is a flatterer.

Surgeons must have an eagle's eye, a lion's heart, and a woman's hand.

There is not a gem in every rock, a pearl in every elephant, sandalwood in every forest, a learned man in every place. —*Burmese*

Those who live near water know the habits of fish, and those who live in the hills can tell the notes of the birds. —*Japanese*

A single flower and a single swallow do not always announce the spring. —*Armenian*

When lions and leopards have left the forest, their place is taken by the lame fox. —*Persian*

The expectations of a dog in a house, and a fox in the jungle are not without success. —*Tamil*

The stag, phoenix, tortoise and dragon are the four chiefs of birds and beasts. —*Chinese*

It is too late to pull the rein when the horse arrives at the edge of a cliff. The time for stopping the leak is passed when the vessels are in the middle of a river.

Unbecoming is a swan among crows, a lion in the midst of oxen, a horse in the midst of asses, and a wise man among fools. —*Burmese*

Every blade of grass has its share of the dews of heaven, and though the birds of the forest have no granaries, the wide world is all before them. —*Chinese*

Be as strong as a leopard, light as an eagle, quick as a goat, and brave as a lion to do the will of thy heavenly father.

Sons and daughters brought up without education are like donkeys and pigs. —*Chinese*

One should know a horse by its speed, an ox by its burden, a cow by milking, and a wise man by his speech.—*Burmese*

The sleeping fox catches no birds. The sleeping cat catches no mice.—*Persian*

You can't catch wild beasts without a net.—*Chinese*

The snake thinks of its hunger, the frog thinks of its fate.—*Tamil*

Even the hedgehog says its young are smooth and graceful.—*Korean*

A hedgehog is a poor bed fellow.

Although a cheetah is sick, it is stronger than an ox. —*Tamil*

Two cats and a mouse never agree in one house.

Sickness comes riding upon a hare, but goes away riding upon a tortoise.

The deer, the monkey, the partridge and the peacock; these four are the thieves of the field.—*Hindi*

The rhinoceros looks up to the moon and wastes this thoughts for that which he cannot have.—*Chinese*

The fish swell in the depths of the waters, and the eagles in the sides of heaven; the one, though high, may be reached with the arrow, and the other, though deep, with a hook; but the heart of a man at a foot's distance cannot be known.—*Burmese*

The cat and dog may kiss yet are none the better friends.

The wolf changes its hair but remains the wolf. However you bind a tree, it will always grow upward. Though you put oil on a dog's tail, it will never become straight.—*Russian*

About Noël-Marie Fletcher

Noël-Marie Fletcher is a journalist/photographer based in Washington, D.C. She is the author of *"Windows into the Beauty of Flowers & Nature," "Pathways in Time: Photo Journeys," "River of My Ancestors: The Rio Grande in Pictures," "Captives of the Southwest,"* and *"My Time in Another World: Experiences as a Foreign Correspondent in China."*

She has lived in Hong Kong, Beijing, and Germany (Nuremberg, Berlin) with a stint in Switzerland. She speaks Spanish, Mandarin Chinese, and French and studied Russian. She attributes her zest for life, analytical abilities, love of adventure and creativity to her unique fusion of ancestors—Spanish conquistadors, English Quakers, and a Royalist navy captain who was a privateer with pirate Henry Morgan.

A native of New Mexico, she is proud of the contributions her Hispanic and English relatives made to help found America.

Her maternal Hispanic family left Spain for the New World and settled near Santa Fe, N.M. Her Perea family, whose members were among the earliest Hispanics to serve in the U.S. Congress (Francisco Perea, Jose Francisco Chaves, and Pedro Perea). The Pereas were important community leaders under three flags (Spain, Mexico and the United States) and leading business entrepreneurs who helped found the Santa Fe Trail.

Her paternal relatives came to America from England, Scotland and Wales as colonists in New Jersey, Pennsylvania, Maryland and Virginia. Many fought as patriots during the Revolutionary War to help establish the United States of America.

Noël-Marie founded Fletcher & Co. Publishers as an outlet for creative writing, illustrations and photography. She is a member of the Daughters of the American Revolution and the Descendants of the Founders of New Jersey. She is shown with her rescue Sheltie named Vito, who brightened her life for many years. She adopted him after he was seized by authorities due to neglect by previous owners. He became very spoiled and lives on in her heart. ❀

www.ingramcontent.com/pod-product-compliance
Lightning Source LLC
Chambersburg PA
CBHW061140030426
42335CB00002B/50